HOW TO GET YOUR OWN WAY IN BUSINESS

HOW TO GET YOUR OWN WAY IN BUSINESS

Quentin de la Bedoyere

Gower

Published by
Gower Publishing Company Limited,
Gower House,
Croft Road,
Aldershot,
Hants GU11 3HR,
England

Gower Publishing Company,
Old Post Road,
Brookfield,
Vermont 05036,
U.S.A.

British Library Cataloguing in Publication Data
De la Bedoyere, Quentin *1934–*
    How to get your own way in business.
    1. Business enterprise. Success
    I. Title
    650.1

ISBN 0 566 02826 3

Printed in Great Britain by
Billing & Sons Ltd, Worcester

Contents

Preface

This book is based on three important experiences in my life. The first is the experience of being a professional persuader. I spent sixteen most productive years selling life assurance during which I learnt many ways of communicating ideas so that they led to effective action; and many families and futures have benefited thereby.

My next experience, by coincidence also sixteen years, has been as an executive in a fine business organization. Here I discovered that the skills of persuasion which I had brought with me continued to be of the greatest value. It confirmed my belief that persuasion is the common stuff of human interaction. We are all in the persuasion business.

The third experience overlapped the other two. I spent nearly twenty years working as a volunteer marriage counsellor for the Catholic Marriage Advisory Council. Marriage counselling is about un-persuasion. That is, it is about helping people to uncover the hidden assumptions, behaviours and emotions in their lives so that they become free to make choices about them. Through this I learnt about persuasion from the other side of the fence. The reader is free to take this book as an account of how to persuade, or an account of how to avoid being persuaded. But I hope he or she will remember that, for the world's work to be done, we all have to live on both sides of the fence.

This book is not a psychologist's account of persuasion in business; I have no qualifications for that. It is a practitioner's account. But I have taken some pains to check my observations and experiences against the extensive literature on the subject. The studies to which I have referred should not be taken as proof of any propositions. Few of them are related specifically to business situations and some appear too thin to bear the weight of the conclusions which their authors draw from them. I have used them primarily as a check for my own insights.

Since a central theme of the book is that our view of reality is often contaminated and partial I should have been at fault if I had failed to look for whatever evidence was available to support or confound my views. In turn, my reading has explained many things to me I had not previously understood, and directed my attention to important aspects of persuasion of which I had been only vaguely aware.

To avoid breaking the flow I have confined references, and some additional comments, to chapter notes at the end of the book, where they may be safely ignored by those who are prepared to take my word for it. In the bibliography I have listed a few books to which I am especially indebted; and I would commend anyone who wants to study persuasion further to read them.

For eugraphical reasons I have ordinarily used the masculine form. Needless to say, from the Garden of Eden onwards, women have been redoubtable persuaders.

Quentin de la Bedoyere

Acknowledgements

My thanks are due to Dr Michael F. Capra, Senior Lecturer in Anatomy and Physiology at the Queensland University of Technology, who read the complete text and suggested a number of corrections and improvements. And also to my wife, Irene, who corrected a number of details and pointed out several obscurities. I should also thank her for putting up for many months with a husband unable to conduct a conversation without continual reference to scientific studies, and for many years with being the principal target of whatever persuasive powers I may have. Neither are responsible for the views expressed in the book, nor for any errors which remain.

Q. de la B.

Introduction

When I was ten years old I came across a small advertisement for a course in hypnotism. It promised me that, in a matter of days, I could achieve an unassailable power over my fellow man. At the flick of a finger, or the dangle of a fob watch, I could bring the strongest will under my control; the universe would be at my feet. But this intoxicating vision required a fee of £5. Not a large sum for the universe, but too large for a ten-year-old boy. Sadly, my father, who I thought, would have been eager to see his son blessed with such powers, was unwilling to fund the venture. I thought of writing to the advertisers, promising them that if they would send the course I would shortly be in a position to hypnotize my father into providing the fee. But I suspected that my father might well prove to be an exception to the rest of the universe, and I abandoned the scheme.

But not the idea. It is part of the human condition to want to be able to get one's own way, to influence others, to make the world as we want to see it. That is why the human race has survived. But if hypnotism will not do, what will? Many years later I was given a clue.

In January 1957 I attended the Pall Mall branch of the Sun Life of Canada as a trainee salesman. I was greeted by Bill Norris, later to become one of the company's senior branch managers, who said to me: 'Do you want to know what selling is all about? If you do, I'll tell you.' And he told me the story of the Jesuit and the Benedictine.

It seems that the Jesuit and the Benedictine were heavy

smokers. And they shared a problem. Given that they had to spend long periods of each day in prayer, they suffered grievously from tobacco deprivation. And so they agreed to discuss their problem with their respective superiors, and report back the following week.

At their next meeting the Jesuit asked the Benedictine how he had fared. 'Disastrously,' he replied. 'I said to the abbot: "Will you give me permission to smoke while I'm praying?" and he was furious. He gave me fifteen extra penances as a punishment for my irreverence. But you look cheerful, my friend; what happened to you?'

The Jesuit smiled. 'I went to my rector,' he said, 'and I asked him for permission to pray while I was smoking. Not only did he give me permission, but he congratulated me on my piety.'

That story nagged at my mind. I could see immediately why the Jesuit had succeeded and the Benedictine had failed. Yet they were both making the same request. What was the difference? One superior was asked to agree to a religious activity being contaminated by a worldly habit; the other was asked to agree to a worldly habit being elevated by a religious activity. One saw the request as negative; the other saw it as positive. And the lesson that Bill was trying to give me was that the salesman, like the Jesuit, can control the way a request is seen by giving the recipient the right framework within which to make the judgement. Bill was right; that story illustrated the essence of persuasion and, in it, lie the seeds of this book.

Business management is about influence, persuasion and power. Unless the manager can induce his subordinates to implement his wishes he cannot manage. Unless he can persuade his superiors to accept his ideas and, through them, affect the course of the business in beneficial ways, he will always be a pipsqueak. He will often wish to have a power like hypnotism at his command, but – in the real world – he must settle for becoming fully skilled in communicating his ideas in ways which maximize the chance of their being accepted; he has to learn how to get his own way in business.

I was once asked, when preparing for a television programme, to give a definition of selling. After some thought, I
said: 'Selling is the process whereby an idea in the mind of
the salesman becomes an idea in the mind of the customer –
with sufficient impact to ensure that action is taken.' I think it
was a satisfactory definition and, with no change of substance,
would also serve as a definition of effective persuasion. From
the cradle, to the ten-year-old boy, to the approach of the
deathbed – politician, preacher, journalist, doctor, trade
unionist, teacher – in our private and public lives we seek
to use persuasion to impose our wills on the world.

Socrates believed that persuasion should not come about
through the influence of people but through the influence
of truth. The rational seeker after truth should be rigorous
and logical in his search, allowing his mind to be swayed
only by the objective argument, and to present such
arguments to others so that the truth might be available to
them as well. He would not have approved of this book.
Fortunately, for I would not wish to be in opposition to such
an eminent authority, he continually neglected his own
principles in this respect. He neglected them because they
did not correspond to reality.

The reality, as I describe in Chapter 2, *Patterns and
Persuasion*, is that the human mind judges information
against the background of what it already contains. The mind
is not a blank sheet of paper but a complex and crowded
system filled with memories, patterns, ideas and attitudes.
The new information is not judged in isolation but against
this background, and in relation to it. Nor does it use the
whole of the system to make its judgements but only those
parts which it identifies as relevant to the particular case. In
the story the Benedictine asked his superior to make a
judgement about smoking by comparing it with his existing
ideas about praying, whereas the Jesuit asked his superior
to compare praying with his existing ideas about smoking.
And the response was different.

Two important principles follow. The first is that identical
information given to ten different people will be judged
against ten different mental backgrounds, and may receive
ten different responses. The second is that it is possible to

communicate an idea in such a way that it is likely to be judged against a mental pattern which will view it favourably.

In order to make use of these principles it is necessary to look at the processes through which people are motivated to action and the main mental patterns which appear to be common to human beings – concentrating on those which are relevant to business decisions within our Western culture. Fortunately psychologists have done a great deal of work on this subject, and Chapter 3, *Moving Minds*, describes this and, through examples, how it may be applied to everyday business. Common patterns are a starting point, but it is also necessary to look at the individual to gauge which patterns, or variations, are likely to predominate in his mind.

Chapter 4, *Persuading the Boss*, takes up this theme, and uses it to describe how one might approach a specific task of persuasion. It looks at ways of detecting predominant patterns and how the presentation of an idea might be organized so as to use these most effectively. And, since the order is important, a framework for making the presentation is described.

But, in business, the individual to be persuaded is part of a larger community, and the culture and values of the corporation will form part of his mental background. Moreover, few ideas which are not acceptable to the culture of the corporation will ever be effectively implemented. So Chapter 5, *Persuading the Company*, examines this question, and the practical steps which the manager can take to cope with this factor. It turns out that there are close parallels between the mental background of human beings and the collective mental background of corporations. Many of the same rules apply – but there are important differences which need to be respected.

Chapter 6, *Projecting Personal Authority*, looks at the manager who is seeking to persuade. It asks why some people appear to have a natural authority to which others respond, irrespective of their real power. It looks at the characteristics of dominance and suggests how they may be cultivated. Psychologists have identified some of the features which tend to make a person and his message more credible, and these are described.

An important pattern, given in Chapter 3, is the herd instinct, which leads us to be unduly influenced by the actions and views of others. In Chapter 7, *Winning and Using Supporters*, I show how the use of this pattern increases the attractiveness of an idea. Other patterns need to be employed to cultivate the allies and supporters who will be enthusiastic in your cause.

Chapter 8, *Supercharging Staff Performance*, examines how the very powerful pattern of self-image can be used to maximize staff performance. Self-image, a theme which recurs throughout the book, largely defines our capacity and motivation to act. While it is built up through many ways, the manager is in a strong position to enable his staff to develop self-images relevant to their work and to achieve, through this, results which can be truly surprising. But no more surprising than the opposite results, if he gets it wrong.

Delegation is the way through which a manager multiplies his effectiveness and influence. Most of us have had experience of poor delegation from the receiving end, yet our own methods of delegation may be no better. Chapter 9, *Delegation Without Tears*, explains the part which emotion plays in delegation and discusses the patterns which are at work. The chapter describes a complete framework for good delegation which, by respecting these patterns, gives delegation the best chance of success.

Presenting ideas to an audience, whether this is to a small group of senior management or to the Wembley Conference Centre with every seat filled, is the ultimate challenge for the manager who wants to get his own way in business. Most people fail that challenge because they do not understand the fundamental differences between making a presentation to an individual and making a presentation to an audience. Yet, with this understanding, even managers with no great natural talent for speaking can be effective in selling their ideas – and in selling themselves. Chapter 10, *Presentations and Reports*, explains audience behaviour and how to make it work for the speaker rather than against him. It gives a complete framework for preparing a spoken presentation which takes into account many of the patterns explained earlier in the book – and some additional ones which apply particularly to audiences.

The final section of Chapter 10 looks at written reports, concentrating on the features which contrast with platform presentations. I have described how to attract the reader and how to make maximum appeal to motivation, meaning and memory. Here, too, the patterns and methods described in the book can be effectively employed.

But to demonstrate the power of persuasion in its purest form I have described the life assurance salesman at work in Chapter 1, *Selling Power*, which follows immediately. It will show you how an expert sets about transferring an idea in his mind into the mind of his customer, so that effective action is taken. He is the aristocrat of persuasion. If you really want to get your own way in business, learn first from him.

1 Selling Power

The life assurance salesman has nothing to show his customers except himself and the power of his ideas. Yet he can more than double his success by using the true principles of persuasion. He can reveal to us the secrets which we can use to double our influence in business.

If you want to know how to get your own way, go to the experts. There are people who spend every day practising the arts of persuasion, and monitoring their skills by the only measurement which counts – getting a signature at the bottom of an order. The life assurance salesman has no goods to sell, no beautifully designed hi-fi to display, no motor car to offer for a demonstration ride. He only has an idea to talk about, and it's an idea which will cost the customer money now for a benefit which he will receive only in the distant future – if at all. No wonder he needs to pay attention to his methods of persuasion; unless his skills are very high, his income will be very low.

Skills that can more than double success

The difference between an experienced life assurance salesman and a trainee is marked. The new man will typically close one sale in seven; the experienced man, one in three. Experience increases effectiveness by over 130 per cent. The same product, the same type of customer, the same basic message – but a great difference in the skills of persuasion.

Can the life assurance salesman teach the business manager how to get his own way in business? You can judge that for yourself by witnessing a sale in action, and understanding the principles which are being skilfully applied. You may never make a life assurance sale yourself but, if you can translate the principles into the context of your own work, you too can benefit from that 130 per cent increase in the power of persuasion which a knowledge of the patterns of human behaviour brings.

First impressions

The sale starts in front of the salesman's wardrobe. In the first moment of meeting, the customer will form unconscious impressions about the salesman's social status, his level of success, his professional attitudes, and whether or not he can identify with him. Clothes are the first message he receives. And the salesman's own feelings will be affected by what he wears. His confidence about his appearance will give him a sense of quiet, dependable authority which will be instantly communicated. These first impressions are important: they colour the whole of the interview, and the sale can be won or lost in less than a second.

> **Trevor Williams, my first sales manager in the life assurance industry, tells me he had a slow start to his career. His branch manager asked him his ambitions and Trevor replied: 'I want to earn a professional man's income.' His manager asked him how he expected to do that when he didn't dress like a professional man. Trevor, who had a young family, pointed out that he couldn't afford the clothes. So his manager lent him the money. Twelve months later he had increased his income fivefold; the loan was repaid and a highly successful career was born.**

One step at a time

The salesman's first contact with a new customer may well

have been on the telephone. He doesn't ask for an appointment to make a sale but only for an opportunity to explain an idea which he thinks will be of interest. He emphasizes that he will take no more than a few minutes and that he will only make a further appointment to present his full idea if the customer is interested. Since he is quick at seeing things from the customer's point of view (the ability to see another's point of view – empathy – is an important quality for a salesman[1]) he knows that the usual reaction to a sales call is fear. The customer is afraid of getting into a sequence of events he can't easily control, with potentially expensive consequences. And so the salesman reassures him about this. By making a modest request for a meeting, and having it granted, he increases his chance of getting the larger request – for the full sales interview – later. Wherever possible he will use a recommendation from a mutual friend, or some other indication of his trustworthiness. Objective evidence is likely to carry greater weight than any statement he makes about himself.

The appointment will be confirmed on business paper. This conveys efficiency and the reassurance of a solid business address. Most life assurance sales take place over a short period of time and an essential factor is the level of trust which the salesman is able to induce. The letter contributes to this, becoming an early brick in the edifice of trust which must be built.

Establishing the relationship

At the first meeting a minute or two must be spent in developing the relationship. The salesman will increase his credibility through establishing that he and his customer have some points in common – perhaps a mutual friend introduced them, perhaps they own the same motor car. He will use good, but not intrusive, eye contact to stimulate liking. (However a woman should remember that males often interpret female eye contact in ways which may not be intended.) And he will look for a sincere compliment to pay; the feeling of well-being this gives the customer will set the tone for the whole meeting.

Jack Bell had many clients in the hotel industry. During an electricity strike he would send in his business card attached to a very welcome candle – almost good for currency in way of the shortage. He told me that this led to an excellent welcome and a high chance of a sale. He had to cease the practice because one night an hotel he visited burnt down. Jack was jumpy for the next week – expecting the police to call bearing a used candle with his name and address attached.

Soon the salesman will suggest that they review his idea. He will have some papers to show the customer, and this obliges them to sit side by side or at least at right angles. It is better to be 'on the same side' rather than on 'opposite sides', and their physical relationship will define their psychological relationship. A good way of conveying an idea is to show simplified details of a life assurance scheme which has been arranged for another client who has similar circumstances to the customer. The client's name will obviously be blocked out, relieving the salesman from the need to state the importance he places on confidentiality. The demonstration will enable the favourable points to be made quickly, and will give the customer a thumbnail overview which will help him to grasp the later sales presentation. And the fact that another client has taken the scheme will be seen as good evidence of its virtues.

Going back on your word

At this point the inexperienced salesman is likely to get himself into trouble. Sensing that the customer is interested, he tries to convert the initial meeting into a sales interview. Thus he loses the advantage of the familiarity and comfort which comes from meeting a person twice; this is more powerful than the familiarity which can be achieved at only one meeting – however extended. And he sharply forfeits trust by reneging on his undertaking about the nature of the interview. With more experience he will remind the customer that any further meeting is up to him, and he will ask if the idea is sufficiently interesting for this request to be granted.

Faced by this strong confirmation of trustworthiness the customer is motivated to agree and, provided the idea shown is relevant, will hardly ever refuse.

> **I was saved from the perils of inexperience in this matter by my inability to do mathematics when watched by a third party. Incidentally this characteristic is shared by cockroaches.[2] I *had* to work out the details of the scheme in private, and sometimes found myself insisting that I was late for another appointment in order to get away.**

Assuming that a further interview has been granted the salesman will ask permission to obtain the details he needs to fit the idea to the customer's individual circumstances. Provided he explains his reasons for this, uses the respect due to the customer's private information, and listens intently and interestedly, he may find out more about the customer's affairs in twenty minutes than any other person has found out in twenty years. Factfinders are now generally obligatory under UK regulations but they have been used for generations by salesmen who appreciate the need we all have to be properly listened to, and know that the sharing of personal information is a most powerful method of building a trusting relationship.

Already a large number of factors which favour persuasion have appeared, and the salesman is only now bringing his preliminary interview to an end. I will not go through the sales interview itself in such detail – but I will highlight a selection of examples which illustrate further principles.

Let the customer do the selling

The salesman is unlikely to waste time convincing the customer that he has a need for the product. Instead he provides a framework in which the customer can convince himself. This anecdote will illustrate the point:

> **I was on my way to a sales interview with a customer who, at the factfinder, had told me that he had no intention of**

making a purchase but – and he was a charming man – he was willing to listen to my presentation provided I would not be too disappointed when we did no business. The thought of an interview doomed to failure in advance depressed me, and I did not bother to prepare for it. At his house the only thing I could think of saying was:

'You told me last time, Mr Strawn, that you wanted a minimum of £20000 a year as a retirement income. I've looked at your existing arrangements, and added in your State pension. Between them they will only provide £15000 a year. How do you propose to make up the difference?'

As I could think of nothing further to say I shut up. After a long silence, while Mr Strawn made some calculations on the back of an envelope, he said to me:

'You're supposed to be the expert. Why don't you tell me?'

By chance rather than design I had discovered that you can rarely persuade a man; you can merely make it easy for him to persuade himself. It took me exactly 50 words to complete that sale – the rest was just simple explanation and completing forms.

Converting objections into questions

The same principle will be used when the customer raises an objection. It's very hard to defeat an objection since the customer's pride is involved. So the salesman never hears objections; he hears questions:

Customer: Yes, I can see that looks like a substantial sum on paper. But it's not going to be worth anything by the time I retire. I mean, in twenty years it won't even buy me a cup of coffee.

Salesman: You're concerned about inflation. How would one ever make sure that the benefits keep their buying power over the years? Is that your worry?

Customer: Yes, that's exactly it.

Salesman: You're quite right of course. But luckily that's not the whole story. You see, as the value of money goes down so does the value of the regular investment you make. And this plan has a facility which allows you to restore your investment level to its original value, and so increase the payout at the end.

Notice how the salesman listens to the customer's point and demonstrates that he has understood it, before he attempts an answer. Only when someone has shown that he has heard our difficulty are we ready to accept his solution. And, far from being shown up as mistaken, the validity of the customer's point is acknowledged, and new information – which the customer could not reasonably have been expected to know – is used to answer his 'question'.

How the bad news can become good news

The salesman might well have raised this point without waiting for the customer. Through doing so he will demonstrate that he is genuinely concerned with giving the full picture – light and shade. This will strongly reinforce the trust which is necessary for the sale to be made.

For technical reasons life assurance policies have low cash-in values in the early years. As a young salesman I avoided this negative point and, whenever I was asked a question about it by a customer, I knew my answer would lose me the sale. My friend Frank Seward gave me the solution: 'Don't wait till they ask. Tell them. Emphasize it. Tell them you want them to realize that it's a long-term investment, that they mustn't start if they don't want to keep it up.' So I told them; and I never lost another sale because of cash-in values.

Transmitting the images

Words carry their own luggage by way of overtones. The salesman in the dialogue above uses the word 'investments' in preference to 'premiums'. 'Premium' carries the overtone of a price being paid; 'investment' suggests a contribution to your own fund from which you will benefit. The good salesman chooses vocabulary which expresses his thought exactly – both literally and emotionally.

The right words can convey the right ideas and they can also convey the right image. To get the decision he is looking for the salesman needs the customer to be prudent, farsighted, and unselfish where his family is concerned. The customer may however be feeling how much he would rather spend the premiums on his present wants, that the future may never happen, and that he would rather put the whole thing off until another day. And so the salesman must help the customer to get the right image of himself, and then live up to it. By treating him as if he were prudent and unselfish, and finding opportunities to imply this, he may well succeed in getting the customer to see himself differently and to behave in accordance with that. A large part of our self-image is formed by what we see others expect of us.

The herd instinct at work

How do you know what size of 'investment' you should properly be making? Without other sources of knowledge you will probably fall back on the short-cut of using other people's judgement. Here's how the salesman puts it:

> **In trying to choose an appropriate level of monthly investment for you I've been guided by what I've found most people in similar circumstances to yours feel they can afford. But don't hesitate to tell me if it's too much or too little – only you can decide.**

In most instances the customer will decide that he can afford just exactly what people in circumstances similar to his own can afford. Why should he be different? And his decision will be made all the easier because the salesman has assured him that he alone is in control of the decision. The moment an individual senses that he is losing control he tends to compensate by fighting back, even against his own interests. Give him control, and he is open to suggestions.

The salesman's time machine

The life assurance salesman faces a difficult problem. Most other salesmen are offering an immediate benefit in return for payment; and in the case of a credit sale the first payment may be very small. The life assurance salesman, by contrast, is asking for immediate payments for a benefit likely to be delayed long into the future. But human beings, and animals for that matter, generally respond much more quickly to immediate benefits – even if they are small, than to remote benefits – even if they are large. To bring the benefits forward in time the salesman will use two main methods. One is the motivational story. For example he might describe the circumstances of an elderly friend who has reached retirement without an adequate pension. The customer, like most of us, will tend to identify with a well-told story: for a few minutes he will become the elderly friend and experience some of his feelings of anxiety about his standard of living. Another is a direct appeal to the imagination: 'Just imagine for a moment that you're aged 60 plus one day. You're sitting in an armchair looking at the gold watch they gave you yesterday. Suddenly you realize that you have perhaps 20 years in front of you and an income that, by your own judgement, is too small to give you the comfort you require. Tell me, what's going through your mind at that moment?'

Closing the sale

More has been written about the psychology of the close of the sale than any other aspect. Only one or two points to illustrate principles will be made here. The object of the close is to get action, not to get a decision – the decision has already been made, though not necessarily formulated, as the interview progressed. What the salesman has to do is to provide the easiest and smoothest path to allow that decision to be expressed through signing a form. Inertia is a powerful ally for the persuader. Make it easier to sign than not to sign; remove the obstacles to completion, and the signature almost writes itself.

The first obstacle is the completion of the form. Forms look so very definite. Brian Reeves had the answer:

> **As a junior salesman Brian attended his first sales meeting, where we were discussing the best way to produce application forms without alarming the customer. Various expert methods were suggested; finally Brian was asked, out of politeness, for his views. 'Oh', he said, 'I get the form out when I first meet the chap. After all I'm going to need things like his date of birth and the spelling of his name as part of my factfinder. I don't see why I should fill them out twice, so the form's already half done before I get to the close.'**

Not surprisingly Brian developed into a brilliant salesman. He had learnt, by instinct, that for the most part people do not notice what they are used to. By using the application form as part of his constant sales equipment it had lost any surprise for the customer.

With form in hand the questions must still be asked, and these can be a further reminder that a decision is being implemented. Unless he is using Brian Reeves's methods the salesman will not start with the customer's name. A name is a sacred, numinous thing; it is best left till later. A more likely opening question might be: 'What would be the most convenient way of making your investment – annually or monthly by direct debit?' The question does not ask the customer to decide about the plan, only to decide between relatively trivial alternatives. A potential obstacle has been removed and the process can continue.

The salesman has one more surprise in store. When the form is completed he marks the space for the signature and proffers a pen. But he does not invite the customer to sign. Instead he says: 'Please check through the form carefully for me, I may have made a mistake. And don't forget to read the printed information at the foot. It's there because it's important.' Just at the moment of greatest fear and tension, just when the customer is remembering his parents' words: 'Don't sign anything until you've read it', the salesman is not only giving him the time to read; he is insisting that he should. What a trustworthy, decent person he is! No wonder that, a few minutes later, a signature finds itself beside the spot the salesman has marked.

Reviewing the salesman's skills

You may find that account alarming. It seems that the life assurance salesman is conducting himself with a deliberate and secret skill to make a sale inevitable. With that equipment at his disposal how does the ordinary, uncomplicated, straightforward person have a chance? But, in practice, two out of three turn down the sale because there is no form of persuasion, short of a machine gun, which can reliably bring about results. All the experienced salesman can do is to raise his probability of success. Second, there is no reason to suppose that the salesman is anything other than completely sincere in what he does. It is true that he could use such methods to achieve dishonest ends, but that is another question. Nor is he necessarily being deliberate. For the most part, at least, he is behaving in the way that his experience has guided him; and he is often unaware of this. You probably learnt quite early that a big smile brings a willing response and a scowl brings trouble. Do you ever take advantage of that fact, even unconsciously?

On the other hand you may feel that the account is a useful defence. The next time you meet a life assurance salesman you will understand his tricks and be unaffected by them. Try it. You may discover that his methods are just as effective whether you know about them or not.

Key principles in action

The salesman placed much emphasis on first impressions. The way he dressed and carried himself and the tone of the initial relationship were important. We tend to make very quick judgements of people, based on immediate information, when we meet them. And generally those judgements persist because we continue to look, subconsciously, for evidence to confirm our original verdict, and to suppress contrary evidence. Of course our judgement can be reversed if the contrary evidence is strong enough, but first impressions carry a long way.

Any sale where two relatively brief meetings will lead to a customer undertaking substantial payments over several years for an intangible benefit, has to depend on trust. Prudence suggests that we need to have known people for a long time, and to have observed them in a number of circumstances, before they can be regarded as trustworthy. In practice we very quickly make a judgement of trustworthiness. It is as if we carried around in our heads a picture, or a pattern, of what trustworthy people do. And when someone seems to act in accordance with that pattern we make the assumption that they are trustworthy. So, by quite simple actions like sticking to his undertaking about the limited nature of the first interview, or emphasizing the limitations of his product along with its benefits, or encouraging his customer to read the 'small print', the salesman conveys trust. Reading this account makes it obvious that such evidence of trustworthiness is quite insufficient for a reliable judgement, but in the sales interview it is enough.

The effects of first impressions and the conveying of trustworthiness suggests that people are given to hasty and superficial judgements. It would be more accurate to say that people normally use short-cut judgements. In the next chapter I will explain why the brain has needed to develop such methods, and why a knowledge of them is so valuable to anyone who wishes to be able to persuade others effectively.

The salesman is concerned that he should handle the transaction with authority and confidence. He does not have the authority which can demand compliance but rather the authority which comes from his expertise and his confidence that he has something valuable to offer. Provided he can communicate this to his customer through his personality and his actions he can make use of the characteristic of inertia which most people have to a greater or lesser degree. If someone with such authority puts forward a course of action we are inclined to go along with it unless some positive obstacle stands in the way. In this example the successful use of inertia at the close of the sale depended on the accuracy of the salesman's judgement that the customer was ready to go ahead provided the way was made easy enough for him.

The customer needs to feel that he is control in order to be persuaded. Tell a toddler not to touch a switch, and watch his fingers stretch out towards it in cautious defiance. It is part of being human to want to be in control, to avoid the control of others. And so the salesman emphasizes the customer's control: it is *his* decision whether the second interview takes place; it is *his* information which defines the need for the product; it is *his* choice of premium level. At no point is he allowed to feel that he is being cornered; even his objections are turned into requests for information before they become a challenge. Motivation is at the centre of getting one's own way in business, but at its heart is the concept that if a man can see a goal ahead of him which is worthwhile in his own terms, and if he can see that the solution offered can best achieve this goal, he will act.

First impressions, conveying trust, the faculty of the brain to make short-cut judgements, the effects of authority on the one hand and inertia on the other, the motivation which comes from the customer's sense of control over events are all key factors in influencing people and organizations in the way we want them to go. Later chapters will put them into the context of ordinary business and show how they might be used. They are not true secrets because they are available to everyone, but they are kept better than most secrets – and anyone who chooses to study and use them will have the power of influence at his command.

Summary

The life assurance salesman demonstrates some of the factors in persuasion in a concrete and concentrated way. The main ones are:

- The effect of appearance and general bearing on his authority.

- The vital role of first impressions.

- Taking persuasion one step at a time.

- The building of trust throughout the transaction, and how this can be achieved quite simply.

- The importance of listening, putting the customer into the driving seat, allowing him to sell himself.

- The importance of the right words, and how imagination can bring the past into the present.

- The use of inertia, and the herd instinct.

Analysing the salesman's methods highlights some key factors in how to get your own way in business. Putting them in a conventional business context and showing how to use them is the purpose of this book.

2 Patterns and Persuasion

If you want to influence the judgement of another person you need to know how that judgement works. The human brain has developed short-cut strategies to cope with the vast amounts of information it receives. Through understanding these strategies it becomes possible to present new ideas so that they are most likely to influence others. The brain works by being very sensitive to new information which it analyses and understands by comparison and contrast with the patterns it has built up from past experience. The manager who seeks to persuade cannot simply rely on objective factual argument; he must present his ideas in terms of the patterns which the recipient has built up. The principles explained in this chapter are demonstrated in action in later chapters of the book.

How hot is a bowl of water? Take three bowls: one of cold water, one of hot water, one of lukewarm water. Soak your left and right hands in the hot and cold water respectively, then plunge them both into the lukewarm. To the left hand it feels cold, to the right hand it feels hot.

When I carried out this simple scientific experiment as a youngster I found it interesting but not momentous. I certainly did not appreciate that I was encountering one of the most basic and important phenomena of the human brain: that we exercise our judgement not absolutely but through change, contrasts and comparisons.

The whole subject of how human beings make their judgements is vast and complex. Even the psychologists for whom this is a life's study would agree that our knowledge is far from complete – although it advances continually. But those who seek to influence others must acquire at least a basic understanding of the forces which are at work. Armed with this understanding it becomes possible to begin to master the arts of persuasion and influence which are central to the work of the effective manager.

In brief . . .

- The brain maximizes its capacity to process information through a very efficient strategy: first, by recognizing new information which is important and by filtering out information which is unimportant; second, by comparing the new information with patterns already in the brain.

- These stored patterns provide our pre-packaged judgements, responses and attitudes – for example, our recognition of the characteristics of certain types of people or useful ways of behaving in particular situations. Some of these patterns appear to be common to human beings, and have probably developed through the needs of evolution; others have been developed through experience. Throughout life we continue to evolve our own individual patterns as we encounter new situations.

- While the brain needs to work this way, the method has its problems. Some of the inherited patterns are no longer appropriate for modern life, and there is no guarantee that the patterns we have developed ourselves are correct or correctly applied. Fortunately the rational human brain is able to override the patterns and check them for objective accuracy. But to do this we have to recognize that there is a pattern at work, and we need time to think more deeply.

- The skill of persuasion largely depends on under- standing which patterns are being used by the person to be persuaded. If new ideas are presented in ways which enable these patterns to judge them favourably, they are likely to be accepted.

A little excursion into the brain[1]

This process of making judgements by comparison and contrast with existing experience does not sound ideal. Surely ideas should be assessed on their objective merits and not by how they relate to what already happens to be in the mind. But, like it or not, that is the way that human judgements are characteristically made. It is not a perfect system and it is constantly open to error but it has evolved through millennia of evolution because it has proved necessary for the survival and development of our species.

The brain faces a big problem – how to cope with too much information. The stimuli which present themselves to our senses are vast in number and variety. There are countless smells available to the nose, countless lights and colours in front of our eyes, countless different noises presented to our ears. Yet we have to respond appropriately to this immense environment – often at great speed, sometimes instantaneously. The fastest and largest computer in the world could only deal with a tiny fraction of the task, but we have to do it with a brain weighing less than a kilogram and a half. To cope with this task the brain uses short-cuts which reduce the processing work, and therefore the processing time, by a very large factor. And the central strategy employed is to compare new information with what is already present; in this way the brain needs only to focus its full attention on the differences; it does not need to waste its processing power on analysing the full situation from scratch. The senses assist this strategy by responding quickly to stimuli which the brain recognizes as an important change, while ignoring other stimuli which are unlikely to be significant for it.

Because of the brain's limited capacity these short-cuts are essential; without them we could make little sense of the world. But there is a price to pay: if judgements are made by comparison with previous experience then their accuracy will depend on the reliability of that previous experience, and whether or not the piece of experience chosen for the comparison is appropriate. And those who seek to influence others must accept that rational judgement and objective assessment of the arguments ordinarily play a rather small part in decisions; much more important will be how new proposals and ideas compare with what is already in the mind of the person who is to be influenced. The positive corollary is that the true power of persuasion lies in the intelligent use of this knowledge.

Recognizing change

Before looking at how the brain accumulates the patterns of experience against which the comparison is to be made, consider a problem which can be very important in a business situation.

Would you consider £5000 a year a generous salary rise? That depends on whether you are currently earning £10000 a year or £100000 a year. If you recommend that your firm should open an office in Switzerland the proposal may go through on the nod if you already have overseas offices in Austria, France and Germany; but if you only have an office in Birmingham you may find that your directors take a very close interest in the idea. This illustrates the fact that the absolute amount of the change is not as important to the brain as the degree of contrast to the preceding situation. Many a budget controller knows the trick of increasing a large budget item by a small relative amount, rather than a small budget item by a large relative amount – notwithstanding the identical effect to the bottom line.[2]

Thus the evaluation of a change, or even its recognition, can depend on non-rational factors of which the decision maker may be unaware. A firm may shy away from a vital decision simply because it involves too big a contrast with its existing habits of business; another firm can fail to notice a gradual deterioration in performance because the degree of change year by year is too small to attract the attention of the brain. A large section of the accounting industry devotes its time to manipulating company accounts (quite legally) so as to show a smooth rise in profits over a period, rather than the sudden fluctuations of real business life. It does so because investors are worried by sudden changes and comforted by smooth progressions – even though few of them can be unaware of what is actually happening.[3] But they may not realize that their fears are founded in inheritance from primitive ancestors to whom sudden change was a warning of approaching danger.

The patterns of experience

The process through which the brain evaluates the new experience in terms of existing experience is simple in principle, although complex in practice. If you show a chess expert a board with the position the pieces have reached halfway through a game he will be able to grasp the situation quickly by making use of the patterns he has stored; he will be able to make an intelligent guess as to what led up to that position and perhaps forecast the outcome of the game. Ask the same questions of someone who does not know the game – and therefore has no stored patterns – and he will be flummoxed. The expert only has to notice and analyse the similarities and differences from the patterns he knows; the non-player, without the patterns, would have no basis for judgement or understanding of what is happening.

Interpreting present experience in terms of patterns built in the past is characteristic of the way the brain works. There are many forms – covering large areas of human experience – as the following examples show.

Pre-packaged judgements[4]

The brain carries round with it a number of pre-packaged judgements which it has incorporated from experience. Faced by circumstances which appear to correspond, the judgement is brought into action. For example you may believe that people with untidy desks have untidy minds. Or that if they have tidy desks they can't be very busy. You may habitually make your purchases on the principle that it is always cheaper in the long run to buy the highest quality available; I may not. You may work on the assumption that people should be trusted until they have proved otherwise; I may assume the opposite.

Stereotypes

Stereotypes are concerned with groups of people who are seen to share certain characteristics. Take the following list: Englishmen, Jews, Irishmen, Italians, West Indians, Scandinavians. You may find that each of those groupings suggests characteristics – good and bad – to your mind. And this means that your judgement about members of the group you encounter are affected by your expectations. But stereotyping goes far beyond such well defined groups; it could cover tall men, blonde women, university graduates, adolescents, homosexuals, musicians – and so on. We hold in our minds assumptions about scores of groupings which provide a starting pattern against which we make judgements about the individuals we meet.

A friend of mine in the advertising industry is fair-haired and slim. He looks several years younger than he actually is. During a salary discussion with his boss he pointed out that his salary was less than that of his contemporaries. His boss was amazed to discover his real age, and made an immediate adjustment to his salary. Another friend of mine, with a misleadingly youthful appearance, has had difficulty in getting the promotion he deserves. Two patterns are linked here. The first is an assumption that young appearance means young person; the second, that youth is not qualified for high remuneration or authority. In both cases the stereotypes have cost their victims several thousands of pounds over time.

Behaviour routines

As a marriage counsellor I quickly learnt how many

relationships are structured, for good or ill, by characteristic ways of behaving. For instance one person may habitually boost their partner by being naturally supportive and generous with praise; another may achieve a different effect through continual criticism. Both may be well-meaning. The managerial type who always seeks to lay the blame on others is well known; so, fortunately, is the manager who ensures that his staff get the credit rather than him. Some like to manage by inducing guilt in their subordinates (and in their spouses); others by focusing on what people can achieve in future, taking little notice of mistakes. These patterns are also learnt from past experience, and save the brain from continually working out new ways to respond by providing routines which have already been mastered.

Patterns from the past

Pre-packaged judgements, stereotypes and behaviour routines are called up by the brain whenever it recognizes a situation for which one of these ways of dealing with new information seems appropriate. They are particular instances of the general principle whereby we use organized patterns of experience from the past to interpret current experience in a fashion which makes the most efficient use of the brain's processing power. An everyday example of this strategy in action illustrates this basic way in which we understand the world, and develop our understanding of it:

Most people have an idea of what is involved in having a formal meal in a restaurant. A table has to be booked, there is likely to be a certain number of courses chosen from a menu, the waiting staff will behave in a predictable way, there will be a routine for payment. And when such an event takes place the brain will not have to process everything which happens as if it had never been encountered before. Instead it notices the differences from the remembered pattern – perhaps that the waiting staff are unusually surly, or that one diner requires only a salad and a glass of mineral water. The brain is following its strategy of efficient processing by attending to the new and only using the old

for purposes of comparison. The battery of remembered patterns grows with experience. The first time you eat a Chinese meal the differences from the familiar pattern are very marked: the atmosphere are different, the taste of the food and the manner of handling it are different; but other elements of the pattern, such as the payment routine, will probably be the same. After a few visits to Chinese restaurants you will have established a 'formal dinner' sub-pattern; this time for Chinese occasions. And now you will be well placed to discriminate between different Chinese restaurants because your new stored pattern will give you a baseline for further comparisons.

Building patterns

The restaurant example shows a common way in which patterns are built, but the influences which act on patterns are many. Evolution dictates a number of ways in which we instinctively react to experiences, and the interplay between our particular genetic inheritance and our early, formative influences will also be important. For example, an optimistic temperament will interpret experience differently from a pessimistic one – and will therefore build different patterns; an intellectual cast of mind will be more sensitive to some stimuli, an artistic cast of mind to others. Parents are influential – through what they say, or by how they behave; and other social influences, including those from reading or television, will contribute.

Patterns are strongly influenced by what is known as the *primacy effect*. That is, an initial, strong experience may dictate or overshadow the resulting pattern. For example, a manager who tries the experiment of employing a rehabilitated offender – who then lets the manager down – may assume for ever after that such people can never be trusted. However, if his first two or three experiments work well, he will be inclined to dismiss a subsequent failure as exceptional. A recruit may form a picture of the company he is joining at his initial interviews, and be strongly influenced by this picture for a long time afterwards.

Many interesting experiments have been conducted to test

this effect. In one, an account is given of a person's character. When the good attributes are given first and the bad attributes second, listeners come away with a better impression of the person concerned than when they are given the other way round.[5] In another, an individual is asked a series of questions. If he gets mostly correct answers towards the beginning, making mistakes towards the end, listeners will judge him to have performed better than if the wrong answers came first, or were evenly spread – even though in all instances the total score was the same.[6] In a third experiment, a $1 bill was slipped into some shoppers' baskets when they entered a store; when interviewed later these shoppers reported their mood as happier and more optimistic than those who had not received a dollar bill.[7] It seems that we are programmed to grasp a situation very quickly, and then to let that grasp influence how we interpret subsequent experience. No wonder the salesman in the last chapter tried to ensure that his first impressions were good.

Closely linked to the primacy effect is what is known as the *recency effect*. This simply means that we are unduly influenced by happenings which have recently alerted the brain. Most people who have just witnessed a road accident will drive more cautiously for a time, although the probability of a further accident has not increased as a result. A manager may well be more influenced by an opinion he has heard that morning than more thorough evidence which is remote in his mind. The salesman in Chapter 1 made use of the recency effect when he asked his customer to check the form carefully before signing it; such an unusual request made a powerful impact at the very time when the salesman wanted to maximize his communication of trustworthiness.

Maintaining existing patterns

The persistence of the primacy effect is one example of our tendency to maintain existing patterns; we don't want to be confused with new facts. By noticing, and recalling, evidence which supports our existing view, and ignoring conflicting facts, we are able to maintain our familiar pattern. Here are some examples:

- Dick Gerachty is a practical, commonsense person who started on the shop floor and reached the top of his company through shrewdness and flair. Reluctantly he was persuaded to recruit a young business school graduate with an MBA. He scarcely bothers to read the graduate's reports – finding them wordy and theoretical. When the graduate does good work Dick is inclined to put the success down to outside factors. But he always remembers the failures – and often quotes them in support of his view that there's no substitute for starting at the bottom and getting one's hands dirty.

- Selection interviews can be a trap because the interviewer is vulnerable to stereotyping. Once an interviewee is mentally placed in a category the interviewer may be more attentive to evidence which supports that, and to ignore what conflicts. Occasionally the interviewer 'remembers' information which was never given, and can only be convinced by hearing a recording of the interview.

- I once made myself unpopular with a colleague by bringing a small computer to meetings so that I could take notes. He said that he found the clacking of the keys extremely irritating. Only when I had demonstrated to him that the keys were completely silent did he accept that his nervousness came from other motives.

- In the US presidential election of 1972 the successful candidate was Richard Nixon; his opponent was George McGovern. Six months later the Senate hearings on the Watergate scandal started. It was established that Nixon voters took significantly less interest in the televised hearings than McGovern voters. It was inferred that Nixon voters wanted to avoid evidence which might suggest that their votes had been unwisely cast, while McGovern voters were pleased to have their wisdom of choice confirmed.[8]

Patterns can be self-fulfilling, too. The MBA graduate will probably leave shortly to work for a more rewarding employer – thus confirming Gerachty's belief that soft college graduates can't take the pace. But before this, his performance may have started to deteriorate because people tend to live up, or live down, to the expectations of others (see Chapter 8). Managers who use an authoritarian – sticks and carrots – style train their staff to respond to this; if they attempt to switch to more liberal measures the staff react by taking advantage, thus proving that the original style was correct after all. Psychologists have coined the term 'learned helplessness' to describe a condition where someone, as a result of critical feedback, gradually deteriorates in performance.[9] Various degrees of this can often be observed in business.

Making the facts fit

We may be amused by the people who maintain that the earth is flat; their ability to resist the evidence for its roundness seems absurd. But it's as well to make sure first that you have not succumbed to the tendency to make the facts fit in some other, perhaps less dramatic, context. It's very uncomfortable to maintain two views which are incompatible with each other, and the tendency is to try to reconcile them. One method, described above, is our ability to avoid noticing the conflicting evidence; another is to avoid asking the questions or making the investigations which we suspect will lead to contradictions.[10] Thus a salesman, knowing that his effectiveness may depend on his belief that his product is competitive, may avoid reading any objective surveys which could suggest otherwise; or an interviewer who likes a candidate may avoid the probing questions which could reveal a flaw.

Some interesting studies have been carried out to demonstrate what is known as 'psychological accounting'. This occurs when someone justifies in their own mind a decision by adding additional reasons which seem to make it sensible. For instance, in a much-quoted experiment, students were asked to undertake a very boring task, and

were then paid to tell other students that the task was
interesting. One group received $20 for this; another group
received $1. The second group, questioned later, reported
that the task was genuinely enjoyable and interesting. It
must have been, mustn't it? After all, who would tell a lie
for only a dollar? The first group reported that it was boring
– otherwise, why would anyone pay them $20 to lie about
it?[11] I know that I'm an opera fan – after all, I accompany
my wife once a fortnight during the season; and I would
hardly do that if I wasn't. A business may judge its success
on a number of criteria, for instance: return on capital
employed, market share, bottom line, financial strength,
loyalty of its customers, new sales, turnover of staff, etc.
Which measurement, or combination of measurements,
seems the most reliable indication of success may depend on
which is showing the most comforting results. And this can
vary from year to year without anyone suspecting
inconsistency – even in themselves.

**A sales manager, who understood psychological accounting
well, had to report to his board of directors that the number
of life assurance applications obtained over the year was
below target. He said: 'We were successful this year in
achieving our premium income targets with fewer
applications, thus relieving strain on the administrative
departments.' The following year, the number of applications
was well ahead of target. Without batting an eyelid he said:
'Despite the many difficulties we face this year, my salesmen
produced a high number of applications – showing the level
of hard work they put into their results. And, in so doing,
they substantially increased our client base – which will be
very valuable to us in the future.'**

Our capacity to apply different standards of judgement is
considerable. A senior politician has recently been in the
newspapers; just as he was publicly criticizing the selfishness
of people who resist new housing developments in their
neighbourhood, it was revealed that he had objected to a
development near his own house. There is no reason to
suspect hypocrisy; no doubt the two situations looked very

different to him. Fortunately our own inconsistencies usually
go unpublished.

Professor Robert Ornstein (see Bibliography) uses the
concept of 'different minds' to explain how we are able to
respond inconsistently to objectively similar situations. For
example, our judgement of others' behaviours may be quite
different from our judgement of our own, since different
segments of the mind, insulated from each other, are
employed. We may not spot the inconsistency until some
intervening factor draws our attention to it. Even then it will
often be more comfortable to leave the insulation intact, by
ignoring the inconsistency or finding some way of
rationalizing it. Blaise Pascal, the French philosopher, said:
'The art of persuading consists as much in pleasing as in
convincing' (*The Art of Persuasion*, 1658). Three hundred
years later it remains true that evidence is rarely sufficient
to persuade; the listener must also be emotionally prepared
to receive it.

The rational override

This brief account of the brain's use of patterns from the
past – the pre-packaged judgements, the behaviour routines,
the stereotypes, the general patterns of everyday life – and
the various ways it has of resisting change by neutralizing
conflicting evidence, is not edifying. Man no longer looks
like a rational animal but a non-rational animal. His
judgements are based on patterns developed long before he
became *homo sapiens*, or inherited from his parents, or built
from scant evidence. Even their development through
experience is heavily contaminated from what has gone
before. Not much dignity there.

Yet the picture is not so black. We have already seen that
the use of patterns is an essential means of enabling the
brain's limited processing power to incorporate new
experiences. You have only to imagine what it would be like
if every changing circumstance had to be evaluated from
scratch without the help of patterns from the past into which
we can fit and understand the present. Prejudice is a word

with unpleasant overtones, yet literally it means no more than prejudgement. The person who is truly without prejudice, if we could imagine that, would stand helpless and dumb before experience he had no means of understanding.

And, for all its limitations, the system works. Any creature which has survived through millions of years of evolution to reach the advanced stage of man can only have done so because, on balance, the characteristics developed have worked well enough to ensure that the line continued. But mankind has developed a further characteristic which enables him to compensate for some of the defects in the system, in a way which distinguishes him from other creatures – the rational override.

Think of the modern camera which automatically adjusts its focus and shutter speed. It will cope with most normal conditions and take satisfactory pictures. But when it is faced with unusual conditions, or when special effects are required, it will not do the job. And so the photographer switches to manual override and substitutes his judgement for the programmed judgement of the camera. The analogy with the brain is clear: the programming through patterns of the past is satisfactory most of the time, but we have the capacity to switch to rational override whenever we need to bring our full judgement to bear. Of course human beings are far more complex than a camera, which has distinct modes of operation into which it can be switched. Human judgements are a mixture of the non-rational and the rational and it's hard to tell in a particular instance which element is the strongest. It is difficult, and sometimes impossible, to stand far enough away from ourselves to be able to distinguish what is rational and objective from what we have merely internalized from the past. If, for example, you challenge my judgement that management requires a strong and authoritarian hand in order to be effective, I can quickly bring arguments and supporting evidence to bear. I may not be aware of all the past experiences going back to my childhood, or even to my pre-human ancestors who hunted the savannah in disciplined packs, which have influenced my conclusion.[12]

And most of the time I will not bother to look. I will allow first impressions to influence me unduly. I will allow recent events to carry greater weight than longstanding or objective observation. I will resist change which requires me to jump too far from the familiarity of existing experience. I will still react by using my accustomed routines notwithstanding their unsatisfactory outcomes. I will continue to pull down pre-packaged judgements from the dusty shelves of my mind. And please don't give me contrary evidence. Even if I notice it, which is unlikely, I will try to interpret it so that I do not have to face the discomfort of changing my mind.

Patterns and persuasion

This system of human judgement is, for good or ill, the one that we have; there is no way of changing it. But we can make use of it – by working with, and not against, the patterns of those with whom we have to deal. We need to make sure that others are using the appropriate pattern against which to compare our ideas, that we present matters so that they relate comfortably in comparison with existing patterns, that when another's pattern needs to be changed or developed we do this skilfully, and that we handle people with the respect which is due to their non-rational as well as their rational nature.

The last chapter provided, through the imaginary life assurance salesman, examples of this in action; and in this chapter many similar examples have been used incidentally to illustrate points. In the following chapters I shall build on these principles, seeing them work in a variety of business contexts, developing a picture of the power of persuasion in action. Meanwhile, here are some further examples which you may like to study. See if you can detect the patterns in action, and think of other examples from your own experience of similar methods of influence and persuasion.

- **When Amstrad decided to market their complete word processor to customers who, for the most part, had never used such equipment before, their selling price was £399.**

Arithmetic tells us that the difference between £399 and £400 is just £1. Why did Amstrad pick such an awkward figure when all their potential customers must have known that the saving on £400 was trivial?

- Life assurance salesmen often illustrate a plan with a premium which includes additional benefits, such as double indemnity for accidental death. The benefits are not mentioned until just before the close – when the customer is inwardly debating whether to make a positive decision. The method is extremely effective. Why?

- A woman who let rooms to lodgers tried two forms of advertisement; in one she showed the total weekly payment inclusive of bills like electricity and gas. In the other she showed the basic price for the room, stating that bills were extra. The second form of advertisement drew substantially more replies, and her lodgers continued to be impressed by the cheapness of the accommodation throughout the many months they usually stayed. Since the total cost was the same either way, how were patterns and comparisons working here to her advantage?

- A brand manager in a consumer goods manufacturing company wanted to introduce some modifications to a product line. She knew that she would have a hard time getting agreement. A day or two before she planned to present her case she received a strongly worded complaint from a good customer – a complaint which the modifications would have solved. With great innocence (that is her style) she took the letter to her marketing director and asked for his experienced help to answer it in the most constructive way. When she made her presentation to the product committee she had scarcely finished her introduction when the marketing director started telling the story of the letter. Her proposals were accepted with little further discussion. What principles had she employed to strengthen the effectiveness of her case?

- Professor Ornstein suggests (rather than advocates) that

a good technique for buying a privately advertised car would be to get a friend to telephone first and offer a very low price. What influence might this have on the acceptability of the modest, but somewhat higher, offer you subsequently make?

- Recently my eldest son went for an interview for a very desirable job in a government department. As the interview started he noticed that both he and the interviewer were wearing Durham University ties. He grinned at the interviewer and said: 'Since we're both wearing the same tie, hadn't we better agree that I've passed the interview already by demonstrating my good judgement?' It was, my son told me, one of the pleasantest interviews he has ever had. And he got the job. What forces were at work here?

Finally, you may have noticed that, in some of the examples, the methods being used to persuade or influence were obvious; nevertheless they remained effective. What does this suggest about people's ability to be rational and non-rational at the same time?

Summary

- Because the brain is limited in its processing power it cannot cope with all the information it receives. Therefore it ordinarily works by noticing changes from the existing situation and analyses the differences. Although this method is very efficient it is also prone to error since its sensitivity to new information is not always reliable, and its knowledge built up from the past – with which comparisons are made – is not necessarily soundly based.

- In making its comparison with existing experience the brain uses patterns which have accumulated from the past. Instances of specialized patterns are: habitual ways of judging situations; stereotyping classes of people into groups with assumed common features;

behaving in characteristic ways. Other patterns are more general and are used continually as the basis for judging new experience. Frequently new experiences modifies the existing patterns or becomes the basis of a sub-pattern from which further experiences can be analysed.

- Patterns are built or modified through evolution, genetic inheritance, social influences and personal experience. Initial experiences may have a strong influence in setting the shape of a pattern (primacy effect); recent experiences may take precedence over past knowledge, even when this is more soundly based (recency effect). However there is an underlying tendency to preserve existing patterns; this may be done by noticing evidence which supports the pattern and ignoring conflicting evidence. We are also good at interpreting evidence in ways which allow us to accept contradictory information without modifying our patterns.

- Human beings possess a rational override which allows them to validate their patterns or overrule them. However, the rational override will only be employed if an individual realizes that the patterns he is using may not be appropriate. It is hard for the individual to decide how much of his judgement is rational and how much is non-rational.

- Understanding these aspects of human judgement is important for those who seek to influence or persuade. By presenting ideas with respect for the non-rational as well as the rational characteristics of the recipient, chances of success are greatly increased.

3 Moving Minds

The secret of successful persuasion is finding out what a person wants, and helping him to get it. But the motives which lead a person to act are complicated to untangle, and they are often not fully understood even by the person who has them. However, some useful theories of motivation have been developed which serve as a starting point for analysis, and there are other common patterns which can help the process. Nevertheless each individual will be unique in his motivation, and the reasons that he gives for his actions are not necessarily his real reasons.

Many decades ago Dale Carnegie wrote: 'So the only way on earth to influence the other fellow is to talk about what he wants and show him how to get it . . . There is only one way under high Heaven to get anybody to do anything. Did you ever stop to think of that? Yes, just one way. And that is by making a person want to do it.'[1]

Why are people motivated to take action? The decision is a result of balancing three factors: the needs or wants we have, the 'price' we are prepared to pay to get them, and how probable it is that our proposed course of action will be successful. Psychologists call this the motivation calculus.[2] In most instances we perform the calculus instantaneously, but sometimes the evaluation will take days or weeks to make. Patterns can play an important part. We have stored, and often unconsciously, ideas of our needs and wants – we don't need to analyse them from scratch. Similarly we may have stable ideas on what we would be prepared to do to achieve a particular goal. Even the way in which we perform the actual motivational calculus can be a pattern. If, for instance, we are habitually optimistic about the outcome of what we do, we need to devote less time to considering the 'effectiveness' element – which we largely take for granted.

> **Recently I was visited by an Australian relation whom I had not seen for over 30 years. In her late 60s, she is studying for a university degree. When I asked her what had led her to undertake this formidable task she reminded me that I had once told her (with all the brashness of my youth) that you could do anything if you had the confidence to do it. The pattern set at that time was still influencing her motivational calculus half a lifetime later.**

Applying this understanding of motivation to discovering how to influence others through finding out what the other fellow wants and showing him how to get it is clearly difficult. If motivation depends so greatly on the patterns stored in the brain of an individual, and if the various factors are so complex, how can one ever hope to understand them well enough to employ them usefully? Fortunately it is a little easier than it appears at first sight. Psychologists who have studied the subject have identified a number of forms of motivation which are sufficiently common amongst human beings to provide useful, though far from infallible, basic approaches. But the need to match motivation to the particular patterns of an individual remains, and – after looking at some more general aspects of motivation – I shall address this problem directly.

Some key thinkers on motivation

The only way to be fair to motivational theorists is to read their own accounts, and I have listed some sources in the notes to this chapter. I propose to be highly selective, picking those aspects which I have found particularly useful and which I have observed in practice. They share two characteristics: the first is that they can only record *tendencies*;

that is, the conclusions can only be based on general observations and may not apply in any specific instance; the second is that such theories are continually disputed or modified in the light of subsequent work, and this means they can never be the last word – they must be studied with a critical eye.[3]

Abraham Maslow[4]

Maslow pictured human needs on an ascending scale: at the bottom are the physical needs like hunger; at the top are the 'higher' needs like self-fulfilment. He argued that the lower needs take priority, and it is only when these have been satisfied that the higher needs become motivators. If a man is starved, he argued, he will not be concerned with self-fulfilment, but only with getting enough to eat; but, when he has enough to eat, he is open to being motivated by the next higher need. Meanwhile the lower need – hunger – ceases to be a need because it has been satisfied. His scale of needs looks like this:

> self-actualization, fulfilment
> beauty, order, aesthetics
> knowledge, understanding, exploration for truth
> to be esteemed, to gain approval, to be recognized
> to be loved, to belong, to be accepted
> to be safe, to feel secure
> body needs, hunger, thirst etc.

The basic principles of Maslow's theory are subject to a number of qualifications, many of which he made himself and many of which have been pointed out by others. But, for our purposes, two characteristics are important. The first is that what will motivate one individual because it matches his place on the scale will not necessarily motivate another whose place is different. And the second is that needs tend to lessen, or disappear, when they are satisfied. For example, money may be a strong motivation for someone who is short of the money for his basic needs of food, clothing and shelter, or for someone who sees that more money will achieve greater esteem and acceptance for him. But it is less powerful, or may have no effect, for someone who already has sufficient money to fulfil these needs.

Frederick Herzberg[5]

Herzberg's Motivation–Hygiene theory was developed from examining the work situation. He was establishing the kinds of factors which satisfied and dissatisfied workers. He discovered that there were two quite distinct families of factors: the first family – recognition, the work itself, responsibility and advancement – was effective in motivating people. The second family – company policy and administration, supervision, salary, interpersonal relations and working conditions – was not effective in motivating people; but, if the factors fell short, they were effective in dissatisfying them. The first family was centred around the performance of the task itself, while the second consisted of factors which affected the environment in which the work took place – and these were called the maintenance or hygiene factors.

For some people this discovery seemed to contradict common sense. For example, it was received wisdom that providing good working conditions would encourage people's hard and dedicated work. Even now, when Herzberg's theory has been established for over 20 years and has been confirmed again and again in practice, many managers reject it in favour of 'common sense' or, as we might say, a habitual and comfortable pattern of thinking which can be sustained indefinitely by not adverting to contrary evidence.

For many years a marketing company had maintained an adequate pension scheme for its large field force. It was then decided to enhance the benefits through a substantial increase in company contributions. Although everyone now had improved pension prospects the change gave rise to many complaints from long-serving members of the field force who realized that, with reduced years of service remaining to them, they would not benefit as fully as their

newer colleagues. In other words, and as Herzberg would have predicted, the negative elements became more prominent than the positive ones, and, on balance, the company's generosity was de-motivating.

It may not be legitimate to match Herzberg with Maslow since their studies were so different. But it looks as if the hygiene factors are related to the lower end of Maslow's scale, and the motivating factors to the higher end. However, care is required because Herzberg was looking at people whose lower needs were basically catered for, and not – as in Maslow – at people in the round. So it is not surprising that the lower needs did not act as positive motivators since these would be taken for granted by people actually at work in normal jobs. However it does suggest that any threat to these needs would induce a strong reaction to defend them.

Douglas McGregor[6]

McGregor described two common and contrasting assumptions which managers made. One of these, which he called Theory X, held that people are inherently lazy and unmotivated. The proper management approach is therefore one of close control exercised through stick and carrot methods. The other, called Theory Y, held that people are naturally responsible and tend to work hard towards organizational goals. The proper management approach is to provide conditions in which people are free to exercise this responsibility and use it both for the good of the business and their own fulfilment – which are one and the same thing. He argued that Theory X managers would, at best, get mediocre performance from their workers, while Theory Y managers would get superior performance.

McGregor's ideas are complementary to Maslow and Herzberg. They rely on the effectiveness of the higher levels on Maslow's scale, and reinforce Herzberg's belief that people are able to find, and are motivated by, self-fulfilment through achieving success in their work tasks. Thus all three point in the direction that the most effective motivations are ones which are internalized and relate to people's needs for fulfilment. Dale Carnegie would not have disagreed since he, less scientifically, had expressed the same thought decades before.

Common personal patterns and their relationship to persuasion

The key management thinkers I have described are dealing with broad tendencies. But psychologists have also noted a number of more detailed patterns which have a strong bearing on motivation – and, therefore, persuasion. I will describe some of the most relevant in this chapter, reserving to later chapters others which are best understood in the context in which they occur. However, I will anticipate Chapter 8 by giving a brief description of self-image because this constitutes a generalized pattern which, consciously or unconsciously, influences so many of the judgements we make.

Self-image

Gerard is an extremely successful salesman. Being paid on commission, he has a very large income. But he pursues a quiet lifestyle, and he shows very little interest in the accolades he receives for his superior performance. But everyone knows Gerard's income because he frequently takes the opportunity to mention it, ever so casually, in conversation.

At first sight Gerard appears to be an exception to Maslow's theory: his income is more than adequate, and yet it continues to motivate him. But this is to ignore the varied forms of self-image which exist. For Gerard, a man's earning capacity is the measure of his true worth; he is defined by his income. If you earn £50000 a year, you are twice as much a person as someone who earns £25000 a year. We do not need to agree with Gerard's value system, nor even speculate how he acquired it, to accept that earning money motivates him because it fulfils his self-image.

Hilary is working very hard for promotion. Is the motivation money or power? No, the motivation is qualifying for a fitted carpet and a cocktail cabinet. In Hilary's firm these are acknowledged symbols of status.

Again, a naive view of Herzberg would predict that work environment, being a hygiene factor, would not be a motivator. But, in Hilary's case it is a self-fulfilment factor – and therefore strongly motivating. As Robert Heller put it: 'One man's hygiene is another man's motivation'.[3]

One life assurance salesman of my acquaintance used the concept of self-image in a very powerful way. He would conduct his factfinding interview with the husband on his own, and then present his recommendations to husband and wife together. At the first interview he would say to the husband: 'Just to make sure I've got the picture right, tell me which category you fall into. You might be the sort of husband who feels that he wants to provide his wife with as much protection as possible because he loves her, and wants to make sure that she will always have a good standard of living. Or you might feel merely that you owe your wife reasonable protection out of simple justice to her. Or you might believe that, if you die, she can fend for herself since it won't be your concern any longer. Tell me, Mr Jones, which category describes your feelings best?' The husband would inevitably claim to be in the first category.

At the sales interview the salesman would turn to the wife and say: 'I'm going to tell you something, Mrs Jones, that I think you'll want to hear. I asked your husband what he felt about protecting you in the event of his death, and he told me he wanted you to have as much protection as possible because he loved you, and wanted to make sure that you will always have a good standard of living. And that's the basis on which I've prepared my recommendations.'

The wife was dewy-eyed, the husband caught in the trap of the self-image he had presented, and the sale was made.

This example illustrates the difference between the self-image we develop internally and the image which we wish to present to others. In fact most of us devote a great deal of energy to presenting an acceptable image to the outside world.[7] Once we have published that image, consistency requires us to maintain it, just as Mr Jones found himself obliged to do.

The published image may not correspond with how we actually see ourselves; it is more likely to be what psychologists call the ego-ideal; that is, the image of what we would really like to be. For most people the distance between the ideal self-image and the one we actually have is not too great – and trying to achieve the ideal is an important motivation. But, if the distance is too large, the gap leads to low self-esteem – a characteristic of some neurotics. Neurosis can be avoided, of course, by coming to believe, mistakenly, that one is actually living up to the ideal.[8] This may be at some cost to one's performance.

A branch manager, who took great pride in the quality of his communication, interviewed a sales representative who was threatening to resign. After the interview the manager told me that all it had needed to change the man's mind was a skilfully conducted motivational discussion. The man had left the interview, he told me, 'bright eyed and bushy tailed – eager to re-start his career.' I did not think it was tactful to mention that the man, on his way out, had asked me to give him the correct form of wording for a resignation letter – which was on the manager's desk the next morning.

Self-image, in all its varieties, is an over-arching pattern through which we interpret or value aspects of experience. The picture which we have of ourselves may be realistic or it may be fanciful, but it defines what we believe to be important because it defines what we see ourselves to be; we are strongly motivated to live in terms of this picture, and we react instinctively to anything which appears to threaten it. The psychologists can give us a useful list of the characteristics of self-esteem as they apply to most people. But, in the end, it is subjective because we esteem ourselves only to the degree to which we live up to our self-images – whatever they may happen to be.

Many of the patterns which follow in this chapter derive
their motivating force from self-image. In Chapter 4, which
gives a practical account of presenting ideas to a boss,
analysis of the boss's self-image – and how it is projected –
is the key to effective persuasion. In Chapter 6 the close
connection between self-image and natural authority is
described. In other chapters the concept is continually
present, at least implicitly. And in Chapter 8 I describe self-
image in the context of supercharging staff performance.
Even the corporation has a self-image, closely paralleling
that of the individual, which defines and limits what the
corporation can do; a great deal of energy (and money) can
be spent in presenting the right image to the outside world,
and there can be a similar tension between the corporation's
ego-ideal and its reality (Chapter 5).

The ownership of ideas

**The 'Eiffel Tower' technique was first explained to me by
Frazer Peacock Studios who specialized in producing tape
and slide presentations for businesses. Their slide of the
Eiffel Tower was regularly inserted into the presentation,
and just as regularly excluded by the purchasing company.
The idea was simple: the studio knew from long experience
that the purchasing company would want to make some
small alteration to the presentation in order to feel that they
had exercised their critical faculties and to increase their
sense that the presentation was their idea. When the Eiffel
Tower was removed the company was satisfied, and the
final version of the presentation was exactly as the Studio
had intended.**

McGregor's Theory Y (see above) suggests that people are
most often motivated by their own ideas. Pride of ownership
commits us to ideas and makes us enthusiastic to implement
them effectively. But this form of motivation is not only
effective with the people you are managing; it works just as
well with people who are managing you. Many younger
executives make the mistake of imagining that their brilliant
ideas will be welcomed by their superiors. But since the idea

was not created by the superior it starts life at a disadvantage. And often it will be necessary to choose between having an idea implemented and getting credit for thinking of it. If you seek to influence you must try to find ways of transferring the ownership of the idea to the person whose support you require. 'No man,' said Dale Carnegie, 'likes to feel he is being sold something or told to do a thing. We much prefer to feel that we are buying of our own accord or acting on our own ideas.'[9] Moreover, if the idea is a radical one, which might involve too large a change from existing patterns, ownership is a powerful motive for changing patterns to accommodate the idea, or to see the idea in a guise which allows it to fit with existing patterns.

There are different ways of transferring ownership, and a distinction may be made between helping people to have the right idea in the first place and getting them to assume ownership of an idea which someone else has actually put forward. In Chapter 1 the life assurance salesman provides a good model of helping someone to have the right idea. You will remember that he asked the customer to define his insurance objectives, and then to list the provision already made. He then highlighted the differences arising from the *customer's* information. The salesman might well continue by agreeing with the customer that they had discovered two or three different needs; this would give him the opportunity of saying: 'Tell me which of those needs is the real priority, as you see it, the one we need to solve first?' *As you see it* – that's the key; he will act on what *he* sees, not what someone else sees. And so the method of preference is to define problems in such a way that the person is most likely to come up voluntarily with the right solution.

Even where the nature of the problem does not allow for this the skilled persuader will prefer asking questions to making statements. One might contrast the statement: 'I think we ought to close the branch in Aberdeen,' with the question: 'Do you think we ought to close the branch in Aberdeen?' and consider which form is more likely to leave the listener owning the idea. It is a valuable exercise to practice putting across ideas *only* using questions. And it is surprising to discover just how effective this can be.

There are several ways of getting someone to assume
ownership for an idea which you have presented directly.
Here are some examples:

- Hitch the idea to a thought or a value which has been
  expressed in the past. For example: 'Mr Crimmon, after
  you'd placed so much emphasis on cost control at that
  meeting in May, I put my thinking cap on. And this
  new accounting system seems really to be an extension
  of what you were saying.' It's almost always possible
  to find a past remark to which a new idea can be
  attached; and it makes it easy for a boss to accept that
  it is no more than the logical outcome of what he has
  already been thinking. And to deny it now would be
  an unacceptable inconsistency.

- Make it easy for your boss to suggest some amendments
  to the idea (Eiffel Tower technique). At least half the
  ownership of an idea is transferred to the amender, and
  the rest can follow in due course.

- Slightly more hazardous, but effective with the right
  person, is the challenge. For example: 'Computerizing
  our ordering system will pay off in the long run, but
  it'll be expensive at the beginning. And I didn't think
  you'd be very keen on that.' Provided your boss feels
  slightly put out by your assumption that he's mean, or
  isn't prepared to invest in the future, he will react by
  grasping the idea with both hands to prove that you're
  wrong.

- If you can get your boss to participate in the idea in
  some active way, for instance, by explaining it to a
  management committee, his commitment will be
  greatly strengthened. It will not be long before you can
  safely refer to it openly as *his* idea, to which you may
  have made no more than a modest contribution.

Loss of control and reactance

Human beings tend to be extremely sensitive to loss of
control; and this may be because losing the ability to control

the environment must have been a major threat for man's primitive ancestors. One way in which this has been explored is by observing that people who are free to switch off noise if they choose can tolerate levels and types of noise which are intensely irritating for those who have no such choice.[10] It can even be a matter of life and death – in one experiment a group of elderly people in a nursing home was allowed to have control over a number of details in their life, for instance, choosing and caring for the house plants in the ward or choosing whether they would watch a film; another similar group had such matters decided for them by the nursing home authorities. Not only was the general liveliness and morale of the first group noticeably higher than the second, but eighteen months later their death rate was found to be half that of the group which had no control.[11] Most of us, fortunately, do not react to loss of control by dying, but we often react by behaving in rather irrational ways – technically known as reactance.[12] If my wife tells me she has invited my great aunt to tea on Saturday and implies that I am expected to attend, I will suddenly find that that particular Saturday afternoon is very important to me for other purposes. It is not dislike of my great aunt which makes me stupidly obstinate, but losing control of my choice of how to spend my free time. Indeed, if my wife says she has told my great aunt that I may not be available – so as to leave me free – I shall probably be happy to be there.

Naturally we all accept a degree of loss of control when we join a business; we expect it to have its own way of working to which we need to conform – that is part of the employment bargain into which we freely enter. And in a general way we accept the right of our superiors to exercise their control over us from time to time. But it is still a sensitive issue; I am, for instance, more inclined to respond positively to a criticism of a project by a subordinate, since I am not obliged to go with it, than I am from a superior – to whose opinion I need to defer. One firm, suspecting that staff were inflating their expense accounts, instituted a complicated system of checks. Two years later it was discovered that the amount of claims had increased by 30 per cent.[13] The senior managers of another firm had never been required to say how many days of their holiday they had taken. In the year when the system changed and they were required to register their holidays several reported that it was the first time for many years that they had taken their full entitlement. At a simpler level we teach children to say 'please', on the grounds of good manners. But 'please' is short for 'if you please'; and more important than good manners is the fact that this acknowledgement, however nominal, that the other person is free to refuse the request, increases the likelihood that it will be granted.

There are important lessons arising from reactance for the manager working with staff, and I shall return to this in later chapters. But they apply with equal force to the person who seeks to persuade a peer or a superior. Present an idea with too much force, leave the other person with their back against a wall – and you are asking for a reaction which is as irrational as mine was to the prospect of being trapped by my great aunt. When the life assurance salesman emphasized to his customer that he was free to accept or reject a further interview he knew what he was doing. And he used the same understanding of fear of loss of control when he proposed the amount of premium to be paid, with the words: 'But don't hesitate to tell me if it's too much or too little – only you can decide.' And so, in most business situations, you should put forward ideas in a way which allows the other person freedom of manoeuvre; this can be implied by your tone of voice or your choice of words – even, in appropriate cases, by the salesman's words: *only you can decide.*

Self-justification in a 'just world'

The characteristic of looking for evidence to support the stored patterns in the brain and of avoiding contrary evidence, explained in the last chapter, works backwards as well as forwards. It has been noticed that people have an inclination to take personal responsibility for outcomes which are successful, but to attribute failure to external causes over which they have no control.[14]

Some years ago I introduced an investment plan which became very successful and made a large contribution to my company's new premium income figures. It was obvious to me that the excellence of the product's design and the skills used to promote it were the main cause – and I did not hesitate to imply this whenever it seemed appropriate. Then the stock market crashed and sales were severely reduced. How could I be blamed for that? And of course the strong stock market growth which was taking place while the plan was being successful was simply evidence of my good timing.

Self-justification enables us to maintain self-esteem, and therefore self-image, an important motivation on Maslow's scale. Threats to self-esteem must be countered vigorously. A common mechanism for this is known as the 'belief in a just world'.[15] It leads us to assume that we have in some way deserved our rank, or our income, or even our good health. By the same argument we tend to assume that others are less fortunate because they deserve to be. Two thousand years ago the disciples asked Jesus: 'Who sinned, this man or his parents, that he was born blind?' These beliefs are comforting because they reassure us that we are safe in our present position: if I possess some benefit through my deserving rather than by chance then I will continue to possess it because my merit will continue; if you are out of work because of some fault of your own then I, who do not have such faults, am safe. But if these things came about through luck then our positions may be reversed tomorrow and I'd rather not think about that.

'Belief in a just world' can have a negative effect in business. One British company was tempted to sell its small subsidiary in Holland because it was losing market share and becoming disproportionately expensive. Clearly, in a just world, the decline must be the fault of the Dutch manager. Giving in to his requests to provide redesigned products to suit the Dutch market would be to throw good money after bad. Eventually the company realized its error, and provided the subsidiary with what it had requested. Within a year it had

become the most productive subsidiary in the group, and its manager was being showered with congratulations.

Our belief that we have controlled past events, through our actions or our merits, reinforces our wish to believe that we can control the future. In an interesting experiment it was discovered that people who had lottery tickets with random numbers would sell them for a low price, but those who had chosen their numbers (say, corresponding to a birth-date) would only sell for a price four times as high.[16] I am told that public lotteries in Australia have increased markedly in popularity since entrants were allowed to select their own number rather than being given one. But this rather absurd belief about the ability to control chance in a lottery is extended and generalized to include a whole range of outcomes. The illusion of control, which gives us comfort, has another important function. If we really accepted how little control we have, how much comes about through sheer chance, we would be tempted to abdicate from events altogether – since there would seem to be little point in taking action. In fact people of a depressive temperament often do have this point of view, and it explains why it is hard to argue them out of their position, since they have reason on their side. It has even been suggested that comprehensive 'expert systems' operating through computers will never be acceptable because the view they would give of outcomes would be too pessimistic for human beings to bear. We keep some of our illusions because we need them. Unjustified optimism is a survival strategy for the human race.

A colleague of mine was trying to take a decision about a course of action. To help him I suggested that he assigned mathematical probabilities of success at each stage; multiplying these probabilities by the value of the outcomes would give him an objective assessment of what he should do. Unfortunately the completed sum demonstrated that he should not take the action he was proposing. 'That can't be right' he said. He went back through the stages and revised some of the probabilities upwards. The recalculation now

supported his favoured course of action. 'Thanks,' he said to me, 'that's a very useful method of making a decision. I feel I know what I'm doing now.' I felt I knew what he was doing, too.

The herd instinct

This instinct is well named. If you move in concert with the herd your chances of being caught by a predator are small – being one among many. If you move away from the herd you attract attention; you can easily be singled out and destroyed. Unless, of course, you believe you are so much faster than the herd that you can escape – leaving your slower brethren as bait. So most people prefer the comfort of the herd, and the greater the uncertainty and the danger the more that comfort is needed. But the safety may be illusory for, if every herd member is watching the others, who is to warn the whole herd that it may be rushing to its doom? The history of business is littered with fashionable strategies which proved with hindsight to have been disastrous. But how could that have been known at the time, if everyone else was following them?

The life assurance salesman used this instinct when he assured his customer that the premium he suggested was in line with that taken by people in similar positions to his own; and it can play an important part in persuading a boss or a colleague to whom being with the herd is an important value.

Len Morrison made a presentation to his managing director to get his agreement to starting a subsidiary which would lease computer services and create additional income. He opened by explaining that his idea would enable the company to get additional revenue for a trivial investment, particularly important in a year when the directors had been critical of profit levels. His MD started listening with interest, but towards the end of the presentation he was still nervous about the company launching into an untried field. 'Luckily,' Len told me, 'I had taken the precaution of preparing a slide which listed four companies, quite like ours, who had already done the same thing. And one of them

**was Chieveley's – and you know how my boss admires them.'
And so Len carried his case.**

Arguably, if the idea were good it would have been better
to have been first in the field; but it may be better to be fifth
in the field and have a comfortable managing director. Len
once showed me a notice over his desk which says: 'If that's
such a good idea why has nobody thought of it already?' It
reminds him of the value of the herd instinct in getting his
plans accepted.

You will have noticed that the salesman referred to people
similar to the customer, and that Len used companies 'quite
like ours' for his slide. The herd instinct can only apply when
it is recognized as the herd to which one actually belongs.
But Len added force to this by choosing amongst his four
companies one which the MD admired. Herds or groups will
normally have a leader; he who wants to be safe watches the
leader and follows him, knowing that the rest will do so too.
Most of us have 'heroes'; they are people we admire and
whom we tend to imitate, and what they do has a strong
influence on our actions. If you want to persuade a man,
find out who his heroes are – it may be an individual or it
may be a competitor company; and, where they lead, he is
likely to follow. Sometimes a man's hero may be close at
hand – a particularly trusted member of his own staff. Get
his support and the battle may be won.

**Elton was an 'ideas' man. His boss had a great respect for
his creativity but was often nervous about his proposals,
particularly the more radical ones. For comfort's sake the
boss placed great reliance on the judgement of his
hardheaded finance director. Elton soon learnt that if his
idea was supported by the finance director it would go
through without difficulty. In fact persuading the finance
director was more important than persuading the boss, even
if the idea had nothing to do with finance.**

The low-ball procedure[17]

Low-ball procedure describes a situation where someone is

asked to commit themselves to a fairly undemanding course of action which later becomes more demanding. The original commitment induces him to accept the new demands even though the total proposition might have been unacceptable in the first place.

> **I bought a specialized very lightweight portable computer which was being sold at a low price. Later I discovered that I required additional memory which could only be bought as an expensive cartridge. Then I needed a cable and a software program in order to transfer the material to a larger computer, and mains adaptor because of the small capacity of the batteries. By the time I was fully equipped I had spent nearly half as much again in extras. Would I have bought the computer had I been presented with the total price initially? I don't know; but once I was committed I had to carry on.**

In that example my commitment was financial; I was not prepared to waste my expensive investment by not completing the job. But it was also emotional. Despite the mounting costs I still saw the computer as cheap; even today, if a friend asks me the price, I tell him the original figure. And my mind had latched on to the idea of convenience which this facility would give me; I was loth to abandon that. The low-ball procedure can have quite an impact on business decisions.

> **When Len Morrison's idea for leasing surplus computer time was approved he started his preparations. Re-scheduling his company's work so that time could be made regularly available turned out to be quite difficult and to involve some costs he hadn't foreseen. He also had to make some staff changes which added to the cost. And during the preparation period the market changed a little, reducing the price they could charge for the service. His MD was saddened by the prospect of diminishing profits, but continued to support the project. Len told me: 'Now it's launched it's going quite well and my boss seems happy about it. But if I'd known what small returns we'd get I doubt if I'd ever have started. Certainly my boss wouldn't have agreed if he'd known.'**

Marketing theory says, quite correctly, that decisions about the future should disregard unrecoverable costs already incurred. Len and his MD should have reviewed the prospects for the business whenever circumstances modified the profit plan – without any reference to emotion and time already expended. But this is hard to do because the brain's natural way of working is to compare new information with the pattern already formed; it requires a real effort to put the pattern aside and to review the value of the project as if it were being proposed for the first time.

Had Len known from the beginning that the results would vary from his initial presentation it would have been dishonest not to have pointed out the facts. But the low-ball procedure has its legitimate uses:

Elizabeth believed that her company needed to employ a professional copywriter to improve the standard of its sales material, but her boss, who was anxious to keep staff numbers down, would not agree. Elizabeth then sought, and received, permission to retain a firm of copywriters to be used on an *ad hoc* basis. She did not see this as an answer to the problem but she believed that her boss would begin to take higher standards for granted once they had been established. At the appropriate moment she would demonstrate that the costs of employing an in-house copywriter would be less than the fees of the outside firm. Her boss's decision would no longer be about the desirability of good copywriting, his brain patterns would already have absorbed this, but about which method of obtaining it was cheapest.

The life assurance salesman, in Chapter 1, used the procedure when he initially requested a brief interview, with the promise that furthur interviews would only be with the customer's agreement. Frank Bettger, one of the great life assurance salesmen, described how he learnt about this: he watched a steamboat tie up at a jetty. No one could throw the heavy hawser needed to secure the boat; instead, a light line was thrown to which the hawser was attached. It was then simple to pull the hawser across by means of the line.[18]

Many people whom we seek to persuade need a light line first; once they've grasped it the hawser follows with ease. Cialdini describes an experiment in which students were asked if they wanted to attend a class (on a subject of interest) at 7 a.m. About a quarter agreed. A second sample was asked – but no starting time was mentioned. The percentage of volunteers nearly doubled. When these were subsequently told about the early start not one withdrew, and virtually all attended the class.[19] You might like to pause for a moment, and think of how that tactic might be used in a business context.

The foot-in-the-door effect[20]

The foot-in-the-door effect is related to low ball, but a slightly different mechanism is involved. Housewives were asked to display a small sign in their window exhorting people to drive safely. Two weeks later they were asked to display a large placard in their front garden bearing a similar message. At the same time other housewives, who had not been asked to display the small card, were asked to display the large placard. Housewives who had agreed to the small card were significantly more willing to display the placard than those who had refused, or had not previously been asked. This remained true even when the placard was about a different subject and the request made by a person apparently unconnected with the first request. It seems that, in acceding to the first minor request, the housewives formed an image of themselves which portrayed them as the sort of people who were interested in social welfare and prepared to commit themselves to some level of action. The second, much more demanding request, was difficult to refuse without destroying this rather rewarding self-image. The other housewives, not having this image to sustain, had no reason to agree to filling their gardens with placards.

Stanley found his boss's indecisiveness frustrating. Quite simple, but important, decisions would be postponed for weeks. Stanley tackled this by beginning, quite subtly, to treat his boss as if she were a decisive person. He would occasionally make remarks like: 'Thank heavens, you know

how to make up your mind.' And he would refer, with approval, to the one or two occasions in the past where a decision had been taken quickly. Before long his boss started to speed up her decisions – providing Stanley with further examples which could be used to reinforce his point.

The door-in-the-face effect[21]

The door-in-the-face effect (sometimes known as rejection-then-retreat) relies on comparison. The principle is straight-forward: present someone with a hard task, and then reduce it to a less hard one; by comparison the second task looks easy. One study to test this involved college students who were approached out of the blue and asked if they would serve for two years as voluntary counsellors at a youth deten-tion centre. Nearly all refused. When they were approached later and asked to take children on a trip to the zoo, a signifi-cantly higher proportion agreed to do so than the proportion of other students who had not received the first request. Further research showed that it was important for the first request to be so large that no one would feel bad about refusing it; and it was important that the second request should be made by the same person. Apparently the second, lesser, request is seen as a concession – and the student responded to this by agreeing to do the relatively minor task. This effect can be applied to business quite frequently:

Linda was anxious to get her firm into the Common Market before competitors. Deciding to learn Italian she asked her boss for three months' paid leave of absence to learn the language. That was quite impossible; her current work was far too important. The following week she told her boss that she had found an Italian course which would take up one day a week. Her boss was delighted to agree, and insisted on meeting all Linda's connected expenses.

Door-in-the-face is satisfactory for the user because he gets what he really wants; it is also satisfactory for the other party because of the concession he feels he has won. This second aspect is often overlooked:

A large organization was finding its staff council difficult. It went to a great deal of trouble and expense to offer staff good benefits and facilities, but the council always asked for more. On the advice of a personnel consultant, they began to offer much less generous benefits, but would eventually accede with good grace to the council's arguments and agree to what they had always intended to grant. The council was grateful for the firm's concessions but let the rest of the staff know how well they had represented their interests. Membership of the council, which had hitherto only been attractive to malcontents, became sought after by quality members of staff.

Reciprocation

The concession perceived in door-in-the-face draws its strength from the instinct to reciprocate. From the missionary with his glass beads to the lover with his bouquet of flowers we use gifts to make us acceptable, likeable – and to put others in our debt. Cialdini (see Bibliography) describes how the Hare Krishna Society were unsuccessful in begging for money until they developed the device of giving a flower to passers-by before making their request. The change in response was dramatic. The gift itself was trivial (the stock of flowers was often replenished from the litter bins where the gifts had been swiftly abandoned) but reciprocation is not a bargaining process; it is an instinctive response to the fact that a gift has been made.

A gift can take many forms. It could be a small favour done, the loan of a book, a piece of valued information looked out especially for the recipient, even a well chosen compliment. In most business situations, the expensive gift smacks of bribery, and is presumed not to have come from the pocket of the giver, but a small gift allows the recipient to tell himself that his reciprocation is voluntary (see *psychological accounting* in Chapter 2). It should be uncovenanted, clearly require some trouble and thought on the part of the giver, and not be seen as part of a transaction demanding an equivalent response.

Linda wanted to book for a conference on the Common Market taking place in Madrid. The fees were large and she would need extra budget. A day or two before discussing this with her boss she happened to hear a radio programme about her boss's favourite composer. Knowing he was out that evening she recorded the programme, and dropped the cassette in casually the next day. The cost of the gift was an old tape, the flick of a switch and a little considerate thought. The reciprocation was three days in Madrid in a luxury hotel.

Fear of loss

Animals in the wild are motivated by their need for survival. They are preoccupied with successful breeding and with obtaining food, and they are preoccupied with avoiding danger. That sex and sustenance are important for human beings is well recognized, less so is the degree of motivation which comes from fear. Yet Maslow's theory sees safety as one of the primary needs, and two of the patterns I have described – loss of control and the herd instinct – include a big fear component. Of course we are reluctant to admit that fear is a motive, and we are helped in this because those who want to use it for persuasion package it carefully. Who would think of shopping as a fearful experience, yet fear is one of the common motives used to persuade us to buy. If an item is displayed at a bargain price it becomes more attractive simply through the fear of losing the saving if it is not bought; similarly, the suggestion that there are limited stocks or that a decision needs to be taken within a short period makes the item more attractive because otherwise we fear to lose an opportunity. People vary in their susceptibility to this kind of appeal, but few of us are completely impervious, despite our scepticism about the warnings. Who has never found himself looking at an item and wondering whether he would ever have bought it, even at a lower price, if it had not been advertised in that way? Certainly these appeals to fear continue to work well in the commercial world, and few people realize the primitive nature of the instincts which call them to respond.

> In 1983 the rumour went around that tax relief on life assurance premiums was about to be removed in the Budget. Although life assurance is not a commodity that people normally rush to buy, the life companies were swamped with so many applications that a number were quite unable to cope. In 1985 it was rumoured that tax relief would be withdrawn from pension arrangements. Once again the companies were swamped – with the biggest pensions boom in history. In 1988 it was announced that a particular facility was about to be withdrawn from a type of ten-year savings policy. It was a rather obscure facility – not one in a hundred people who already owned a policy would have been aware of its (very small) significance. Sales of this type of policy had been declining for some time, yet the demand to beat the deadline was so strong that we were obliged to close the books early to give us time to prepare the policy contracts before the last day. No wonder that a colleague said to me: 'We really don't need to bother about marketing; all we need is a Chancellor of the Exchequer who will withdraw another facility whenever business is slack!'

Fear is a big, and often damaging, component in personnel decisions. Many important issues are avoided because of the possibility of unpleasant confrontation. In one study nearly 90 per cent of middle managers felt that conflicts were seldom coped with, and two-thirds thought that the biggest outstanding problem in their organizations was the unwillingness of senior management to deal with inter-group rivalries and lack of cooperation.[22] One may often see people left in positions for which they are unsuited, only to hold up company progress for years, and with many other careers damaged in the process. Good reasons can always be given for hesitating to act but the fact is that we are often more scared of challenging the situation than we are of leaving it unchanged. The true circumstances are often only revealed when management consultants are brought in. Providing we can shelter unpopular decisions behind the authority of another's advice we don't seem to mind hurting people at all. In Evelyn Waugh's *Vile Bodies* the publisher makes all his unpopular decisions in the name of his partner – 'old

Rampole'. Rampole himself, having retired to the country
some years before, is never seen. But he's very useful.[23]
Fear is a powerful motivator in persuasion, often more
powerful than the attraction of a positive benefit. But, just
as in the advertisement, it needs packaging. Here are some
examples:

- **'Dave, I know you think that starting up in Europe means
  a lot of work for little reward. But the other side of the
  question is that Continental companies are undoubtedly
  going to come over here and take a bite out of our market.
  Unless we bite back we could find ourselves in difficulties
  five years from now.'**

- **Cialdini (see Bibliography) tells how his brother, Richard,
  made a good living when a student, selling secondhand
  cars. He would give all the enquirers the same
  appointment time. As the first enquirer was making his
  critical examination the second would arrive, and be
  asked to wait his turn. If this pressure was not sufficient
  to force a quick sale, the arrival of the third enquirer
  would certainly do the trick.**

- **'Chessingtons are very keen to have our business, we're
  a prestige account. But we'll have to make our minds up
  soon – I've heard on the grapevine that they're having
  informal talks with Moonstone. We don't want to be
  pipped at the post.'**

- **'Yes, it's certainly a risk opening up a new plant so far
  North. But if we don't we're likely to price ourselves out
  of the market with our manufacturing costs. So there's
  risk whatever we do; it really is a question of choosing
  which risk we prefer.'**

Fear is a powerful motivator, but it needs to be used with
care because it can easily trigger irrational reactions. The
animal response to threat is to fight it or to fly from it. If
the threat is too strong and too immediate, the action taken
may be born of panic and possibly inappropriate; but if the
threat can be accepted calmly and dealt with thoughtfully

then effective actions should result. The examples give instances of pitching the threat at a level which avoids over-reaction but is strong enough to influence decisions: the danger is presented truthfully and in a factual way – and left to do its own work without embellishment. The last example illustrates the value of fear to counter a fear which is already present. Because the human brain tends to judge by comparisons the two competing fears largely cancel each other out, and the decision will be taken only on the balance between them.

The personal agenda

The motivations and the patterns I have described in this chapter cannot be applied indiscriminately. Any one individual will respond in different ways according to the unique blend which is stored in his brain. One person may have high self-image which he will protect fiercely; another may have considerable tolerance for loss of control. One person may respond well to low-ball procedure; another may place little importance on the ownership of ideas. But what I have described will serve as a starting point – a framework within which to judge the particularities of an individual. Thus they will act as patterns for *you* – helping you to reduce your brain processing by allowing you to judge variations from known patterns rather than to analyse from scratch.

Within the more generalized patterns lie detailed patterns which are highly individual. These build up into what is often known as the personal agenda or the hidden agenda. J. Pierpont Morgan once said: 'A man generally has two reasons for doing a thing; one that sounds good and a *real* one.'[24] If that sounds cynical it may be because most of us prefer, most of the time, to hide our own agendas even from ourselves. You may like to try this little exercise:

Presumably you are reading this book because you want to increase your skills at getting your own way in business. You could have a number of reasons for this:

- you believe in the business and want to make it prosper through the benefit of your ideas
- you want promotion
- you have a great need to control things
- your spouse is disappointed in your progress
- you want an office on the executive floor
- you want a good jumping-off point for your next job
- you are after a life peerage
- you want to do better than your brother
- you are less likely to be made redundant if you play a big part in things.

Decide, being quite honest with yourself, how many of those reasons make at least a contribution to your motives for reading the book – and what other reasons, not mentioned in the list, apply in your case.

Unless you are very different from the rest of the human race, you will recognize that you have several reasons – and not all of them are reasons you would care to advertise. If I am to persuade you to read the book I will certainly present the first reason – you're going to need one that sounds good. But don't be surprised if something that I say brings to your mind other reasons which turn out to be the ones that really get you reading.

I have a hidden agenda; and I think you have one, too. So does everybody. Find out what a man really wants, and you can show him how to get it.

Summary

- Motivation calculus is the model which some psychologists have suggested for analysing motivation; it has three elements: the need or want to be fulfilled, the 'price' to be paid in fulfilling it, the effectiveness of the means proposed. If these elements give a positive balance, action takes place.

- Maslow, Herzberg and McGregor have proposed influential theories of motivation. While different motivations will influence at different times, modern work conditions mean that the 'higher' motivations – self-fulfilment, responsibility – can be most effectively invoked. But discrimination must be used as their application is not universal. In particular, the constituents of self-image can vary widely.

- Self-image, the way we see ourselves, has a powerful influence on the potentialities and limitations of our behaviour. The image which we publish is likely to be an idealized version of this – and must be maintained to be consistent.

- An idea is most likely to be embraced by the person who feels he owns it. Prompting a person to think of the idea, asking questions rather than making statements, building on the person's previous statements or wishes, transferring ownership by inviting modification of the idea, are all effective methods.

- Human beings are highly sensitive to loss of control, and they may react irrationally to any threat of this (reactance). Therefore persuaders should use direct or indirect ways of reassuring people that the decision is in their hands.

- Self-esteem depends, in part, on the belief that we are responsible for our successes, not for our failures. A belief that everyone gets their just deserts in a 'just world' gives fortunate individuals a sense of security, which may be illusory. We like to think we can control future events, and this may be necessary to spur us on to action.

- Most people like the safety of the herd, and many daunting decisions are only taken because others have pioneered. People are often influenced by their 'heroes' who may be outside or inside their organizations.

- Low-ball procedure uses for its success the tendency of people to stick to their original commitment. If the benefits are subsequently reduced they may remain committed even though they might not have accepted the modified idea had they known about it in the first place.

- Foot-in-the-door relies on self-image. People who, by agreeing to a modest request, come to see themselves with a new image are more likely to accede later to a much larger request which is consistent with that new image.

- Door-in-the-face (rejection-then-retreat) starts with a large request which is refused. This is followed by a smaller request which is seen as minor by comparison. The reduction in the request is also seen as a concession calling for favourable reciprocation.

- The instinct to reciprocate is triggered by a gift. The gift can take many forms, but should be small and personal. The level of reciprocation does not bear a relationship to the value of the gift.

- Fear is a very strong motivation which is frequently used as a marketing device. It can be used for persuasion in an ordinary business context but care must be taken to avoid an irrational reaction. Presenting a balance of fears can be a useful way of getting the right decision.

- The examples of motivation patterns described are general; each individual has his own variations. And for most people there are the reasons which sound good and the real reasons. Understanding the personal or hidden agenda – using common motivations as a starting point for analysis – is where good persuasion starts.

4 Persuading the Boss

Previous chapters describe many of the main patterns which affect motivation and persuasion. Here, an example taken from business life is used to demonstrate how they might come together in the presentation of an idea. The principles of preparing for such a presentation are given, and a structure for the presentation itself is laid out. The outline principles described apply to a wide range of circumstances.

Understanding the patterns which influence people is an interesting subject in itself, but putting them into action is what this book is about. The circumstances, the ideas, the personalities potentially involved are so various that it is impossible to provide more than a basic account of this process, leaving you the task of gradually increasing your skills and experience. In this chapter I shall provide some outline principles and, using an example, demonstrate them in action. For brevity I shall describe the person to be persuaded as the Target, but bear in mind that persuasion is not a form of attack; on the contrary the idea is to help a person to see how their own objectives can best be promoted through sharing your point of view and making it their own.

Outline principles

- **Know your Target.** Building on your previous knowledge of the Target, try to get inside his skin. See the proposal from his point of view; identify his likely reactions.

- **Review your proposal in terms of the Target.** Identify the Target's patterns and see where they will be relevant to your proposal. Identify the key patterns which will help or hinder you in your task, relating these to the motivation calculus.

- **Decide the order of presentation.** The basic sequence of a presentation is important. Understand why this is so, and fit your proposal to it.

- **Prepare contingency plans and responses.** Try to foresee how the presentation will go in real life; think how you will deal with different reactions from the Target. Sensitize yourself even to the responses you cannot foresee.

The proposal

You are the publicity manager of a long established life assurance company which distributes its range of products through its own field force throughout the country. Your market share has kept pace in a quickly expanding market for a number of years, but you would like to see it growing against competitors. Traditionally the company has not spent much money on advertising, believing that promotional expenditure is best focused on the field force.

Recently you carried out some public awareness surveys which showed that the company was not at all well known in the market, and was often confused with competitor companies. The field force itself frequently complains about low public profile, arguing that this makes its job harder. However, suggestions that sales support money should be diverted to advertising are not popular with senior management. You have now carried out some surveys amongst your policyholders and established that the company has an excellent image in their eyes, and that the majority would buy further policies from you as the need arose. In their answers they make frequent reference to the quality of the sales representatives who look after them – the care they take, the absence of pressure, the convenience of having a trustworthy adviser.

You believe that you have the basis for a large-scale advertising campaign which would communicate an image of a caring company whose representatives are able to help the public make good buying decisions about financial services in a helpful and trustworthy way. Such a campaign would need to be national and it would need to centre on television. With your advertising agents you have sketched in a campaign which will cost about £1.5m in the first year, and £1m annually thereafter.

It is quite clear that this money cannot come from existing profit levels; it can only be provided from the increased sales the campaign would generate and this, in turn, would require an increase in the size of the field force. This will mean asking the company to invest large sums over a period of years before the returns can be expected. You have done some careful projections which show, on your assumptions, that the investment will eventually give a worthwhile profit and substantially re-position the company in the market. But it is quite impossible to prove; the connection between increased publicity and increased sales is indirect, and your faith that the outcome will be worthwhile is not easily communicated.

Your task is to convince your managing director of the merits of your proposal. Such a large investment will require board approval, and getting your MD firmly behind the idea is an essential first step.

Know your Target

In order to persuade your MD, Sheila Robinson, to your point of view you have to know her point of view first. What is her hidden agenda, what is her self-image, what really motivates her? How can you link your ideas into her stored patterns so that she judges them favourably? What elements are likely to contradict her patterns, presenting her with a change which signals danger?

Over the period of time you have been associated with your MD you should gradually have built up a general picture of what makes her tick. While you will have used the principles and patterns provided in the previous chapters as a starting point for analysis, your concentration has been on how she has behaved in the past. Although people can change, and can behave uncharacteristically, the best indicator of the future will be the actions of the past.[1] And this is not necessarily the same as what they have *said* in the past, but what they have done. What people say tells you how they see themselves, or how they would like others to see them; what they do tells you what they really are. In Sheila's case, for instance, she presents herself as a rather hard-boiled, demanding boss; but you know of a number of occasions when she has allowed events to depress her – and lead her into unwise decisions. Without doubt she is a socially ambitious person; she likes to be seen in the right places and in the right company. She belongs to a number of industry committees, and journalists have learnt that she is always good for a strong quote on industry matters. This does not always make her popular, but she puts this down to resentment at her evident success in a man's world.

She is an actuary by professional training but, when she took her present position, she determined that she would become a marketing person. She took a course and mastered the vocabulary; but her knowledge does not run very deep and, under pressure, the actuarial discipline quickly reasserts itself. She is inclined to make little stabs at new ideas, but at heart she is happier working in familiar ways. It is wiser to avoid getting into an argument with her; she has an exceedingly quick mind and has a habit of leaving people feeling rather foolish. However, she is open to reason if handled carefully, but obstinate if not. You like her, but you treat her with caution.

The empathy exercise

Against this general background you now need to consider how your advertising proposal will strike Sheila. Remember, it is not how it strikes *you* that matters, but how it strikes *her*. To do this you must try to get into her mind; that means using the empathy exercise. You carry this out by shutting yourself into your office, closing your eyes, and imagining that you are Sheila thinking about the proposition. You put your 'Sheila' reactions into the first person, and speak them aloud. This is how the first few minutes of the exercise might sound:

> 'This idea scares me. It's an enormous sum of money which is going to leave a nasty hole in the balance sheet. And the risk! Everyone's going to be watching me – and there'll be quite a few only too pleased to see me trip up. What happens if it doesn't pay off? After all I've only got Bob's word for it; and you know these publicity people, they think advertising spend is the answer to everything. And even if it does pay off, that'll be years into the future; and the whole time I'll be wondering about it. Besides, even on Bob's projections I'll be close to retirement by then.
>
> 'Still I've often told myself that this company ought to wake up. It could be much larger, much more important. If it all worked out I'd really have proved to them that I could do it – I'd have a real voice in this industry. And I wouldn't have to wait too long for that; once the market sees a company doing exciting things it sits up and takes notice. The field force would approve, too. They've never really liked having an actuary in charge; now I can show them I'm really on their side. It's going to take a lot of courage, but then I've got plenty of that, haven't I? . . .'

This initial extract from what would be a much longer monologue demonstrates the idea. Notice how little of it takes place around rational judgement, and how much is concerned with the hidden agenda of feelings, self-image and instinctive responses. Sheila will, of course, bring rational judgement to bear, and given her background and personality, you'd better be well prepared for that; but the best case in the world will not get by unless it is presented in the right way. The empathy exercise is an invaluable means of getting on to the Target's emotional wavelength; through role-playing the person, rather than by simply noting what you think they think, it is possible to get much closer to them, and often your imagination will discover aspects you had never suspected. You will also develop a greater sympathy for the Target, and an understanding of his or her situation which will enable you to approach the task of persuasion as a friend and not as an adversary.

Reviewing your proposal in terms of the Target

In just those two paragraphs of the empathy exercise there are several patterns identifiable. I will point up some of these, and you will be able to find others. The first one that strikes me is that Sheila's judgement is going to be largely influenced by her self-image, and only indirectly by the good of the company: she will ask herself whether the campaign will get her into the position of success and influence she wants, or whether it will leave her with egg on her face. Fear plays a big part here, and her actuarial background has taught her never to walk out on a plank without being able to see both ends. Do you think that ownership of the idea will be important here, or do you believe that Sheila will be content to let you get the credit? Then there is the timing question: she wants her reward quickly but the proposal will not pay off quickly; will the prestige of the campaign itself, which she will get in the meanwhile, be sufficient – particularly when set against the worry she will experience before the full benefits appear? The projected new cost is large enough for her to recognize it as a sudden change, especially in view of her naturally conservative approach; the costs will damage the balance sheet and reduce profits in an obvious and highly quantifiable way. But the return will be gradual – and therefore easily overlooked. And although she sees herself as a marketing person she realizes that, in the end, she will have to depend on her evaluation of *your* judgement; and she has a pattern in her brain about advertising people which makes her sceptical.

Identifying the key patterns, as I have demonstrated here, is not difficult to do providing you have observed the Target carefully and seen the proposal in your imagination from his or her point of view. The descriptions in this book of how patterns work and of the main ones likely to apply will become even more valuable to you as you develop your knowledge further through observation and experience. But beware of analysis for its own sake; its sole purpose is to help you identify the patterns which you can use in practice. Being able to anatomize someone's psyche in comprehensive detail may be an interesting hobby, but it can also distract you from the purpose in hand. Don't try to be too clever.

Applying the motivation calculus

Evaluating what part these several patterns may play, and deciding which ones will be the most important, is made easier by using motivation calculus which I described at the beginning of Chapter 3, as a framework for analysis. In this case the main **need and want** to be met, which, for short, we might refer to as Sheila's ego, is quite strong; clearly you must build on that; but the '**price**' to be paid is also high because Sheila's fears will play a big part. How can these be allayed? The **effectiveness** of the campaign is undoubtedly the weak link and, while this may be strengthened, I would recommend, in this instance, that you concentrate on getting a strong positive balance between need and 'price', thus reducing the importance of effectiveness as a factor. Since the outcome of the motivational calculus is a balance between three factors, the weakness of one factor may well be compensated for by the strength of the others.

> **The balance in the motivation calculus can easily get out of hand. Robert Heller (see Bibliography) recounts many anecdotes from big business where needs and wants have so predominated that no real thought has been given to whether the 'price' is proportionate, or where projects were undertaken which, in hindsight, never had a chance of being effective.[2]**

Handling the patterns

The ego pattern needs to be approached with subtlety; you will hardly make progress by pointing out to Sheila directly how important this success will make her. Your emphasis will be on how important this success will make the *company*, and the influence it will be able to bring to bear on the industry. This is another instance of Pierpont Morgan's distinction between the reason that sounds good, and the real reason. Sheila, like most of us, has two self-images: her private one, and her ideal one for publication. Both are powerful levers, and the best course is to present an idea in such a way that both are satisfied at the same time. If you have any doubts about Sheila's ability to make the connection you might commiserate with her on the inevitable increase in those tedious public appearances which the company's success will bring. Your presentation of this point will have to appeal to her imagination if it is to bridge the time gap and let her feel immediately a flavour of the satisfaction she will obtain. However, you will certainly want to emphasize the earlier rewards of leading an exciting company. You may have been fortunate enough to secure a slot for her at a forthcoming industry conference – the title you have in mind is 'Preparing for Future Growth'. And, as you will point out, the media is always interested in expensive advertising campaigns; it's how their salaries get paid. A mention of the enthusiasm of the field force for such a programme will be appropriate here; this will, for instance, be a good subject for her to talk about whenever she visits a sales branch.

The 'price' involved in the calculus will be a challenge for you. It's really quite difficult to make £1.5m sound like a trivial sum. But there are several approaches you can consider. Your first job will be to get it out of her 'cost' pattern and into her 'investment' pattern. Since Sheila is an actuary she will want to see good cost/benefit figures and some testing of outcomes on differing assumptions. At heart actuaries only believe other actuaries, so get one of the company actuaries to check your figures, and mention you have done so. Some people like to see lists of figures; others like graphs. You should know Sheila's preference, and follow it.

Figures have a very strange effect on some people. My former chairman, Tom Galt, held that it was impossible to produce a graph without editing, and therefore

contaminating, the data by doing so. But then he had the kind of mind which could read the meaning of a list of numbers just as some people can hear a symphony by reading the score. The company president, Jack Brindle, also had an eye for figures – and he could spot an error at 20 paces. However, finding an error gave him enough pleasure to look on the rest of the proposition benignly. I would have been tempted to insert an error for the sake of his goodwill, had I not already been prone to making them through inadvertence. More usually, people are simply comforted by having a set of figures like a talisman in their hand. They do not feel the need to check them either for accuracy or appropriateness – they just need to be told what they mean for their magic to work. Nowadays some of the more complex calculations are done, with relative ease, on computer spreadsheets. This enhances their magical potency considerably, particularly for those to whom computers remain a closed subject. The next generation of management may be familiar with new tools, but I suspect that figures will continue to work their magic.

Once Sheila is firmly evaluating your proposal as an investment she will be using the pattern through which you need her to see it. A complementary approach will be to get the sum of money into proportion. Perhaps it's only a small percentage of the total marketing budget; perhaps it represents the profit on a relatively small business increase; perhaps the effect it may have on retaining the field force through raising morale will enable it to pay for itself quite quickly. There will usually be some basis for comparison which will reduce the significance of the sum. And you will, of course, have the estimated advertising budgets for some rival companies available to demonstrate that your proposal is generally in line with the herd.

Fear will be an important element of the 'price', you suspect. The reduction of the psychological size of the investment will have helped here; but you need to do more. An obvious tactic is the herd instinct, and you might develop this from your list of competitors' advertising budgets. This could be reinforced by having some cuttings from the industry press showing respected competitors following the same strategy, or even an industry survey showing a general increase in advertising spend. Presented in the right way this will give her the comfort of being with the herd, and at the same time suggest that there is danger in falling behind. But you will need to be careful in case you remove the motivation she will obtain through seeing herself doing something exciting and new. So you may prefer to handle the fear factor by presenting an opposing fear which will cancel it out. If you can find a way of showing her that in today's market you cannot stand still – either you go forward to new heights or drop back into insignificance – you may change the question in her mind from: 'dare I take the risk?' to: 'which risk do I prefer to take?'

Around one boardroom table the discussion was about salary levels. The personnel director had suggested that the company should raise these in order to recruit higher quality staff, and retain the existing staff. The managing director winced; and pointed out that the budget was already tight enough to squeak. But the personnel director made the point that losing staff and waiting until new staff had been recruited and brought up to speed was a greater, though hidden, cost than new salary levels. The managing director was no longer being faced by just one cost, but a choice between two – one of which was inevitable. He settled for the new salary levels, and left the meeting feeling rather pleased at the cost saving he had achieved for the company.

You will need to think about ownership issues. Given Sheila's character these are likely to be important; and since she must convince the board, her own belief in the project must be complete. However it may not prove to be too much of a problem since Sheila, having taken her marketing course, has often spoken eloquently to you of market share [3] Now you can capitalize on all that patient listening and enable her to see that this proposal is merely the logical outcome of her own principles. But be careful how you put this; if someone like Sheila feels trapped she will retaliate – loss of control is a sensitive issue for her. Would it be possible to present your information so that she herself comes up with a publicity solution? Your task would then be to provide her with the ammunition to take her idea to the board.

This analysis could continue, but we already have more than enough material to use. However none of the thinking we have done so far will be wasted: you will employ it, perhaps subconsciously, to influence how you manage the presentation; and it will sensitize you to react appropriately to the unforeseen.

Deciding the order of presentation

Many years ago I spent some weeks making joint sales calls with a man named Clive. It wasn't a very successful venture because Clive would start his sales presentations by talking about the premium the customer would have to pay to obtain the benefits Clive was about to unfold. Predictably the premium remained the most important thing in the customer's mind, and even when Clive was given enough time to explain the benefits, which wasn't often, they didn't impress. The Clives are still with us; only today I received a proposal whose opening line was: 'I would like to invite Sun Life of Canada to contribute £90000 to the sponsorship of the XYZ Theatre.' I never read the second line. The order of presentation is important and, although it will vary in details according to circumstances, be sure you know what you are doing before you abandon the well established principles.

The order is logical: having set the right atmosphere of optimism, you must capture your Target's lively interest before you get into the substance of the presentation; next, you must establish the need to be fulfilled in such a way that the Target wants to fulfil it; then, you must show the Target how the need is to be met; finally, you must get action and commitment from the Target – that's the only way you know you've succeeded. Imagine a presentation in which any of those steps is omitted; or imagine one in which they come in the wrong order. How successful do you think it would be? Obvious and logical though these steps may seem, too many good ideas lie discarded in the dust because their advocates got it wrong. In order to remember the steps I use a mnemonic – OPENS ACTION. It seems appropriate because if my idea OPENS ACTION I will have succeeded.

O stands for Optimism. You must try to set an atmosphere in which the Target is inclined to look positively at what is presented. Remember the dollar bill in the supermarket trolley (Chapter 2); remember the trouble the salesman took to get a favourable initial impression (Chapter 1). Approaching Sheila you might prefer to pick a day when she has had some good news – perhaps just after the field force has completed a good month. This will give you a topic of conversation to get her looking on the bright side. I once knew a man who took a great pride in his pedigree borzois; a few moments' early chat about the dogs was worth many minutes of logical argument later. Wouldn't it be convenient in Sheila's case if you were able to show her a recent newspaper cutting in which she had figured?

P stands for Primacy. The primacy effect (Chapter 2) occurs when the brain is jolted into attention or lively interest by new information which carries impact. Coming at the beginning of a process it tends to influence the pattern which follows so that it is seen in terms of this new information. The degree of impact must of course be appropriate – bursting into tears in Sheila's office in order to communicate your distress about the company's low profile may be counter-productive. But, to provide a more likely example, you might consider showing her four or five competitor companies who have increased in market share over a period, contrasted with your own company's flat market share. Your words might be: 'I'd like to talk with you, Sheila, about how we can overtake those companies in the next five years.' Do you think she'd give her lively attention to that? If you've chosen the right tactic, the primacy effect will operate and the prospect of beating the opposition will dominate in her mind and influence her reception of the discussion.

Remember that the primacy effect applies not just to the whole presentation but to the separate parts of it. Each idea which you discuss is likely to have its pluses and its minuses; and you will often need to give both in order to establish your trustworthiness. If you want the idea to be accepted, put the pluses first; if you want it to be rejected, reverse the order.

EN stands for Establishing Need. If you seek to persuade you must first get the Target to see that he has a need, and wants to satisfy that need badly enough to accept that the 'price' is worth paying. The need may be positive – something the Target wants to gain; or negative – some loss the Target wants to avoid. And 'want', here, does not ordinarily mean a new want but a recognition, conscious or unconscious, that the proposal meets an existing want. 'Wanting' is an emotional matter; most of us can think with our brains of many needs we ought to fulfil; but it is only when the need in the brain turns into a want in the heart that we take action. The empathy exercise and the analysis of the patterns most likely to influence Sheila which you have carried out will enable you to present a fully logical and reasoned case in such a way that she is most likely to grasp the need and to relate it, by links of which she may not be aware, to what she really wants. And so it ceases just to be an objective need that the company has, and becomes a subjective want that Sheila has.

S stands for Steps to a Solution. The Target has to realize what has to be done to meet the need and resolve the want. And the motivation calculus is completed by recognizing that the steps will be effective in bringing this about. Here again adapting the presentation to the Target's patterns will help the 'price' to be paid to appear in due proportion to the need being fulfilled.

ACTION stands for ACTION. It is fortunate that the word has to be spelt in full to complete the mnemonic because the action step can be so easily overlooked. Yet action is what cements the decision – the equivalent of the signature at the bottom of the life assurance salesman's application. The parallels are close; it is only necessary to translate them from the formal sales interview into the orthodox business situation:

- The salesman will often offer an additional benefit, positive or negative, as a spur to action (recency effect). This might be the best time to tell Sheila about the place you have secured for her on the platform at the industry conference, or that you have negotiated a special 'introductory' deal with a television company provided it is taken up quickly.

- The salesman aims to offer reassurance at this time. You might point out to Sheila that the pilot campaign will incur only minor costs, and that she can review the results before the big costs start. She may well be prepared to commit herself to £¼m of initial costs since this now looks quite small when compared with the £1.5m already planted in her head. This is foot-in-the-door procedure so, to encourage the sense of a concession which needs to be reciprocated, do not offer this too early. Wait until Sheila has grappled unsuccessfully with the thought of committing the larger sum, then suggest the lesser alternative with good grace.

- The salesman tries to get action through a minor question: 'would you prefer to make your investment monthly or annually in advance?' You might say: 'do you think we should use our normal advertising agents or take this opportunity to make a change?'

The action step is not only important for making the decision; it can also be used to confirm ownership and commitment. Anything that Sheila actually *does* to further the idea will be helpful. For example, if she accepts your suggestion that she should look over the outline campaign and see where she might improve it, you have every reason to believe that ownership has been transferred. If you can induce her to take some public action which proclaims her ownership, such as her talk at the industry conference or even an announcement to senior colleagues, you will greatly strengthen her commitment, which will then have been bolstered by her need to maintain consistency.

Contingency plans and responses

Necessarily you have planned the presentation of your idea from one side only, although you have been careful to anticipate Sheila's perspective. But you will be fortunate if it goes through just along the lines you expect. Sheila may not respond as you have foreseen; she may think of objections which never occurred to you; she may have information about company circumstances that you do not know. To prepare yourself for this, take a moment for another imaginative exercise:

Imagine the presentation actually taking place. See yourself sitting with Sheila and starting to set the atmosphere. Think of the different ways Sheila could react to each stage. Suppose, for example, that one of the borzois died during the night, or that at the recent board meeting the directors were very anxious about increasing expenditure. How might you react to that? Think about additional arguments you might use – perhaps keeping a powerful point in reserve to tip the balance at a difficult moment. Do you have compromise positions? What will you do if she tries delaying tactics?

Thinking through the possible course of the presentation will not enable you to anticipate every twist and turn it may take, although it will help you prepare for the more obvious hazards. But it will sensitize your mind so that, whatever Sheila's responses, it will work quickly. Other information you have about Sheila, and arguments in support of your idea which you have not even articulated, will be immediately available to you. I do not know the mechanism through which this operates, but I know that it works. Think the presentation through in your imagination, and you will be readier to deal with even the difficulties your imagination has not foreseen.

Dealing with objections

You must expect the Target to make objections at points in the discussion; if he didn't you might wonder whether he was really listening. Remember that objections are often an expression of ego; the Target does not want to be seen to be persuaded too easily. In fact they are usually signs of encouragement; the Target is really saying: show me how you solve this one, then I'll be ready to listen to your next point. In Chapter 1, the salesman deals with an objection by turning it into a question. And he is careful to clarify that he has understood the objection properly. A danger of careful preparation is that you don't hear the real objection, but only the objection for which you have prepared yourself – this is an instance of being tripped up by your own patterns. Should you hear an objection to which you have prepared an invincible answer, try not to sound invincible; a little hesitation pays proper respect to the ego of the Target, and makes your answer more acceptable. Glance back at the way the salesman handles an objection; it will apply equally in your discussion with Sheila.

Dealing with the contrary argument

Through your analysis of the Target's perspective you will be aware of possible counter-arguments which will be in the forefront of his mind. Broadly, your approach should be to raise these quite early in the presentation, and either deal with them or signal that you propose to do so. Otherwise it is possible that they will distract the Target from your main message. And if they arise towards the end of the presentation their negative potential may be enhanced by the recency effect. But if you think that the Target is generally favourable to your idea, and that the counter-arguments can be easily demolished, you may do better to leave them unmentioned. This gives the Target the opportunity to raise them as objections in due time, and thus allow him to feel that he has toughly debated the matter before agreeing to your proposal. I return to this question in Chapter 10, when dealing with presentations to an audience, where, of course, the speaker has more control over the order of events.

Mind your language

In Chapter 1, I wrote: 'Words carry their own luggage by way of overtones.' The English language is remarkable for its richness, and often allows for a choice of word or expression according to the flavour which the speaker intends to convey. The two versions of the same statement which follow are both saying the same thing. Or are they?

> **'The modern advertising executive is full of creative ideas which can turn a rather staid image into something new and exciting. He knows what aspiring consumers want and he makes sure that the product really fits their expectations. He makes the best use of the latest scientific and psychological methods to ensure that a client's major investment in publicity gets the very best return. After all his fees depend on satisfied clients.'**

and

> **'The trendy advertising guy touts the latest gimmick needed to turn a respectable product into a slick package. He's on to the yuppie wavelength and knows just how to appeal to the punters' greed. He'll describe the current, fashionable theory of consumer behaviour, with a good sprinkling of psychological jargon, and suggest that you can safely bet a fortune that it'll work for you. Win or lose, he still gets his cut.'**

I'll leave it to you to decide between those two descriptions. But it's worth spending a minute or two analysing the methods they use to convey totally different impressions. What is the difference between 'creative ideas' and 'latest gimmick', or between 'major investment' and 'betting a fortune'? The contrast is exaggerated in order to make the point; but it reminds us of the importance of the choice of language needed to appeal to the right patterns in the Target's mind. Care must be taken to avoid giving the wrong impression, or endangering the impact you intend.

> **The selection of effective emotional language seems to start very young. My three-year-old grandson quickly grasped that the phrase 'I want' was counter-productive. He switched instinctively to power language, as in: 'Granny, I *need* a Ghostbusters' gun.'**

The right use of language may be important at several points in your presentation to Sheila. Which choice of phrase, for instance, would have the best impact in support of your case: 'Sheila, our awareness surveys tell us that the public simply don't know that the company exists,' or 'Sheila, the surveys suggest that the public don't yet recognize the important place we hold in the market'?

The use of analogy

Early in her period as prime minister, Margaret Thatcher used the picture of a household balancing its budget as an analogy to explain her approach to the economy. Just as a household cannot afford to carry on living above its means, she said, neither can the United Kingdom. The device is simple, but invaluable. By using an experience familiar to all of her listeners she gave them a pattern through which to understand her policies. No longer did we see the economy as a large, amorphous and apparently inexhaustible resource; we now saw it as something within our own experience and obeying the same basic rules. (I am only speaking of the effectiveness of the analogy; I am not qualified to comment on its accuracy.)

In building your presentation, consider how good analogies could be used to reinforce or explain a point. For example:

> **The way I see it is this, Sheila. Most of us perform better when we feel self-confident. I know I do. And my self-confidence really gets a lift when I hear good things about myself. I think businesses are just the same. When the staff and the field force see the company boosted on their television screens, and their friends start to talk about the**

advertisements, they're going to feel proud. That means better performance all round. So advertising is not just a matter of getting us better known to the outside world; it will give our whole business an image we all want to live up to.

Frames of reference

An effective way of changing the pattern through which an idea is judged is by suggesting a different frame of reference. The salesman in Chapter 1 uses this method when he asks his customer to look at the importance of pension through the eyes of an elderly person, and, in the presentation you are preparing, you may need to get Sheila to see the advertising budget as an investment rather than as a cost. The method can be used extensively and effectively. For example:

> **'Let's just think about this from the salesman's angle, Sheila. There he is, just about to start off on his calls when he picks up the evening paper. And he sees a picture of his own managing director who is making an important comment about the industry. Do you think that will help his confidence? And isn't it possible he'll find an opportunity to show it to his customers?'**

Persuasive listening

(I have described the art of listening at length elsewhere [*Managing People and Problems*, Gower, 1988]. Here, I will summarize the key points as they apply in the process of persuasion.)

Paradoxically the most persuasive people may be those who say the least and listen the most. Imagine that someone is presenting an idea to you. Instead of rattling on continually about its merits he gives you plenty of opportunity to express your thoughts, and really listens to what you have to say. What happens? First, the atmosphere changes: you feel more relaxed; it becomes a discussion between adults and not a contest. You begin to feel good because this other person is really interested in your opinion – and you have warm feelings towards anyone who seems to respect your views. You don't feel hurried, and you don't feel you may be losing control. When you want to think about something he's quite content to sit silently while you do so. If he disagrees with something you've said, you know that at least he's taken in the point you're making. In such an atmosphere you're more inclined to listen yourself, and to find reasons for agreeing rather than disagreeing.

If you feel like that when someone listens to you, why should your Target feel differently if you listen to him? Do you think that Sheila, whose ego needs we have already noted, is more or less likely to accede to your proposal if she feels you have genuinely listened to her point of view?

Good listening is difficult because we are all, by nature, inclined to be much more interested in our own thoughts and what we want to say than in the other person. To listen well this focus must be switched. The listener is trying with his ears, his eyes and his imagination to grasp what the other person is saying – and to see the circumstances as the other person sees them. His body language, including the use of his eyes, will indicate interested attention. From time to time he will make little mirror summaries to communicate that he has understood, or to give the speaker an opportunity to clarify his meaning. He will give the speaker space to express himself, and allow him silences for thought.

The habit of good listening is hard to acquire and easy to lose. Fortunately there are plenty of opportunities for practice. Try some good listening the very next time someone engages you in conversation; you may be surprised at the result.

Summary

- Despite the difference in situations, there are outline principles for preparing a persuasive presentation which you should always try to observe.

- **Know your Target.** Call to mind what you know about your Target's patterns, judged by what he does rather than by what he says. Use the empathy exercise to see the proposal from his point of view; get inside his emotional skin.

- **Review your proposal in terms of the Target.** Identify the main patterns (positive and negative) which are relevant to your proposal; check these against the motivation calculus. Consider how you will respond to these patterns in your presentation.

- **Decide the order of presentation.** Remember the mnemonic: OPENS ACTION. Create an **O**ptimistic atmosphere to help the Target to see things positively. Use the **P**rimacy effect to ensure the Target's attention is caught, and that he will see the presentation in terms of this. Establish the **N**eed in the Target's mind so that it becomes a want in his heart. Show him the **S**teps to a **S**olution which will be effective to bring it about, and which conform to his patterns. Get ACTION to cement the decision, and to develop ownership and commitment in the Target.

- **Contingency plans and responses.** Think through the possible courses the presentation may take, seeing it in your imagination. Note potential difficulties and prepare yourself. This exercise will also sensitize you to react appropriately to the unforeseen. Remember that objections can be an exercise of the Target's ego, and also a favourable signal. Turn them into questions, and do not be too slick with your answers. Decide whether you need to deal with counter-arguments by raising them yourself early in the presentation, or by leaving them to be raised by the Target as objections.

- Watch the emotional loading of your language, plan the use of good analogies, and see where you can use changing the frame of reference effectively.

- Finally – learn to LISTEN.

5 Persuading the Company

So far the main emphasis in this book has been on persuading individuals. But in business the individual is a member of a community which has its own stored patterns, making up the corporate culture and the corporate agenda. These will not only influence how the individual will see an idea, but it will also define which ideas will survive to fruition. Corporate cultures can be broadly classified into three main types, but the more detailed picture of the agenda can only be discerned from careful observation of what the organization values in practice.

If you could be a fly on a wall where would you settle to find out what is really happening within an organization? No, not in the boardroom – that is where people talk about what they know ought to be happening, a place of fantasy not fact. The washroom is the place. Perhaps Freud could explain why people 'come clean' in washrooms, but this is where the revealing anecdotes get told, the corporate in-jokes (which are funny because they are uncomfortable) are made, and where people speak the truth. Here you can learn about the company's hidden agenda. You will find that in many ways it is similar to the individual agenda; it has stored patterns developed through its own history, and it uses these for short-cut judgements just as the individual does. It even has a rational override, through senior management, but this is typically less effective than for the individual since the corporation has a stronger in-built resistance to change. The storage of patterns is collective; they are held within many brains and personalities, and enshrined in the institutions and structures of the organization. And they are inherited through the traditions and habits which pass, almost invisibly, as one generation evolves into the next.

Understanding the corporate agenda is as important as understanding the personal agendas of those you seek to influence. First, the patterns of the individual in the organization are likely to be strongly influenced by the corporate patterns, and any interpretation is likely to be incomplete without this further dimension; second, it is very hard to beat the corporate agenda: you may be able to convince an individual of your point of view, but that conviction will be empty if the corporate agenda stifles the new idea. And, if it doesn't fit, stifle it, it will – although it may be weeks or months before you see your brainchild, to which many people have paid enthusiastic lip-service, engulfed by the corporate maw and swallowed without trace. And you cannot hope to change the agenda so that it is hospitable to your idea; as with an individual, you must modify the idea to suit the existing patterns, or present the idea in a form which the patterns will favour. But, to do that, you need to understand the corporate agenda first. Then you can use it.

Corporate cultures

Dividing the culture of corporations into three main types gives a broad classification which is a useful starting point. Real life organizations will never conform exactly to these, but it is usually possible to place them roughly within a category before examining the finer detail of the agenda, that is, the ways in which the organization behaves to achieve its conscious or unconscious objectives, against the background of its culture.[1]

The Greek temple

The pillars of the temple represent the chief functions of the organization – each one strong and distinct in its own right;

and the pediment represents the overseeing layer of top management, coming to an apex with the chief executive. Temples are made of stone; they are strong and long-lasting. And they don't change much. Large companies naturally adopt this shape when they operate in stable markets where products have long life cycles and methods of distribution are well established. Functions and routines of operation are tried and familiar; individual jobs are defined in terms of the function to be performed rather than in terms of the individual personality of the jobholder. Radical thinking is not popular since it interferes with routines which are known to work; and excellence is measured by the satisfactory fulfilment of the defined function. Over-performance in a job is likely to be as unpopular as under-performance. Intelligence is less highly valued than reliability and thoroughness.

By some standards a temple organization is dull. And, except for the inhabitants of the pediment, it does not demand too much from staff. And so it tends to recruit and hold people who are satisfied by the security it offers, and the comfort of known and relatively undemanding functions. This can be a problem since promotion tends to be on length of service and previous position rather than on merit; thus the inhabitants of the pediment are likely to be those who are products of the system, and elevation will not necessarily change their accustomed way of doing things.

Provided that the conditions in which the temple organization took up its shape – stable markets, little product change, reliable distribution – remain, the organization will continue to prosper; it grew that way because it was the most efficient form for the purpose, and it will wisely resist attempts to alter its culture. But when conditions change it may not recognize what is happening because, like individuals, it instinctively tries to preserve its existing patterns by ignoring or misinterpreting conflicting evidence. But, even when the change in conditions is recognized, it may have difficulty in responding appropriately. Its staff will have personalities and expectations unsuited to change, and the collective traditions and values may be in conflict with what is now required.

The network

The emphasis in network organizations is on skills and focus on the task rather than on hierarchies and functions. Team work which operates across functional boundaries is the preferred method of working, and teams naturally accept, and want, responsibility for their task – rather than to play a small part in a large collective endeavour. Network organizations are flexible and respond to change quickly; they attract intelligent and resourceful people with egos which are strong, but not so strong as to prevent them working within teams and sharing joint responsibility.

The senior management of network organizations is primarily concerned with guiding priorities and objectives so that they contribute to the overall plan, and supporting this with correct allocation of resources. However, frequently changing tasks – and consequent re-formation of teams – has to be handled well if demarcation and coordination problems are to be avoided. When things go badly, or when resources are scarce, frustrations quickly emerge amongst those who are accustomed to a broad control of their own destinies. Previously cooperative relationships become soured by jealousies and histrionic egos come to the surface. The management may well find themselves wishing for the stability and discipline of the temple culture, where individual expectations are not so high, and instructions call forth obedience rather than argument.

The culture of the network organization is attractive, and it accords well with the theories of motivation described in Chapter 3. But its inherent instability requires very skilled management on a constant basis if the talents and independence of its staff are not to lead to disorder. And many people who find the idea of working in such organizations attractive may find the reality is too demanding. They would be wise to leave before they are invited to.

The spider's web

At the centre of the web lies the power; it may be an entrepreneur who has built the business from scratch, or a family firm which still retains tight control over operations. Authority is rarely completely delegated and the whole web responds to the spider's pull. The success, or survival, of staff will depend on their compliance, and those who stay for long periods must be prepared to subordinate their independence without much hope of ever succeeding to power – unless they can qualify as a member of the ruling group. Such organizations are usually small because growth means loss of control as the business becomes more complex.

The advantage of centralized power is to be able to move quickly, decisively, and in a focused way. This can be crucial for new ventures or extremely competitive markets; and it works well when the leader is strongly admired and trusted by his staff. It is also its disadvantage, because wrong decisions will be more damaging. The personal agenda of the power figure is also the corporate agenda, and members of the organization need to realize that this is what they are, for good or ill, supporting.

Cultures within cultures

Even corporations which can be placed squarely within one of the three categories will often contain sub-cultures of a different type. A network organization may have a mini temple culture in its administrative area, and a temple organization may have a business development area which operates on network lines. Mystery cultures,[2] which are formed by people who share a professional skill which distinguishes them from the rest of the organization, are a common sub-culture – for example, the legal team, or the investment managers. The loyalty of such teams tends to be towards their own profession rather than to the organization, and career advancement will be obtained by job changes rather than by waiting for dead men's shoes. Mystery cultures can go to some lengths to insulate themselves from the rest of the organization. They may arrange to be housed in a separate building or, in the case of the computer department, develop a literal insulation through the need for special air conditioning and security of data. A friend of mine who heads a large computer operation, but does not himself have a systems background, told me that he only obtained a passkey into the computer room with the greatest difficulty.

Such sub-cultures often erect a metaphorical insulation through building up a mystique. If the work undertaken by a particular group is so complex that no ordinary person can understand it, how can it be supervised? That group alone can decide what can and cannot be done, and, if their work is sufficiently crucial, they can spread their indirect control throughout the whole organization.

For many years I accepted that the mystique of actuarial work was impregnable. Then I found myself in charge of an area in which actuaries had traditionally predominated. At first I found that my questions about the work were brushed aside. But when I announced that I would approve no decisions until I had understood them, the actuaries sat me down with great patience and began to explain. To their surprise, and mine, they were able to explain the principles (though not all the mathematics involved) with great clarity. Soon we were able to have intelligent discussions about their work, and it was possible for me to provide facilities which made it even more effective. And I was able to defend their point of view against other executives who had made up their mind that the only function of actuaries was to hold up progress.

The preservation of culture

The stored patterns of an individual are hard to change, and this is why persuasion is best done through using the patterns rather than confronting them. I have suggested that changing the corporate culture is even more difficult since it is held collectively and transmitted from one generation to another. It is valuable to look at this in a little more detail.

Cultures breed people; people breed cultures

I have suggested that a given business culture tends to be staffed by people who are suited to that culture. This is one important reason why cultures are so difficult to change. The process through which this happens is easy to understand. Several factors play a part:

- When there is reasonable choice of employment people apply to firms in which they think they will be happy. That is, they are likely to join a culture which suits their temperament.

- Over the years the principle of the survival of the fittest operates. (The 'fittest' does not mean the most excellent, but the most suited to survive in the environment.) Those unsuited tend to leave, those suited tend to stay. Thus the core of long-stayers consists of those who fit the basic culture.

- Communities or groups build common standards and values over a period of time. Teenagers, South American tribes, Western yuppies each have sets of beliefs and behaviours to which their members conform; so do businesses. The pressure to conform to the reference group ensures that, except for a few rogue independents, new entrants are quickly shaped to the culture – and become its upholders.

It is interesting to observe whether the different professions attract and retain predictable characteristics. You would expect that people who are authoritarian by temperament and have a degree of internalized righteousness would be attracted by police work. Similarly, those who are nervous about the big wide world and would rather remain in an environment they can control might move straight from being scholars into being teachers. And those who are uncomfortable in their dealings with the opposite sex might find a profession like the clergy attractive. Those who enjoy solving people's problems from a base of impregnable knowledge might choose to become medical doctors. Those who would rather comment than commit themselves could see journalism as a possible profession. But it might be more valuable to ask yourself what mix of characteristics led you to the work you now do, and the kind of organization within which you do it.

The psychological contract

The relationship between staff and management is broadly common to all organizations; that is, the management has the right to hire and fire, to require specific hours of work, to expect reasonable functions to be performed to a reasonable standard. Correspondingly, management must provide reasonable work conditions, minimum wages and other requirements which are often imposed by law. Yet, behind this, organizations vary widely in the character of the work relationship; this is sometimes known as the psychological contract. It grows out of custom (related to the needs of the culture) and creates expectations which are no less powerful for not having been defined. In one firm the silent understanding may be that you will have steady work with job security, in exchange for a civilized management style and average pay. In another the contract may require frenetic work and long hours; in exchange there is little job security, tough management and high earnings. Sometimes the structure of the pension scheme formalizes the understanding. A scheme which heavily rewards the person who stays for a lifetime and penalizes the early leaver or late entrant indicates a different psychological contract from one whose scheme is easily portable, and different again from one which provides no scheme.

The importance of the psychological contract becomes evident from the degree of disruption when change is attempted; even introducing what may seem minor variations can mean real trouble. Remember the power of reactance (Chapter 3). This can be seen most clearly in trade union disputes, since here protest is formalized; but similar, less organized, resentment and loss of morale can be the result of a change which seems insignificant to a management which does not understand the power of the stored patterns of the psychological contract.

Physical structures

The pension scheme provides one example of a formal reinforcement of existing culture, but physical structures are a tangible reinforcement. The existence of an executive suite, the separation of dining arrangements, various physical marks of status, open plan or closed plan work areas, the whole look and atmosphere of a building contribute. It's not surprising that a change of premises is often seen by management as an opportunity to change culture; but this is unlikely to work since it is only a strand, although a strong one, in a whole rope which binds the culture together.

The senior management agenda

If the measurement of a personal agenda is what people do rather than what they say then there will often be a discrepancy between the wish of management – or even its declaration of intent – to change the corporate culture, and the actions which are taken. And why not? Senior management is an outcome of the existing culture, and therefore comfortable with it. Change may be attractive, but it is frightening; it threatens loss of control and unpredictability. Besides, senior management is likely to be older, with the prospect of retirement in sight. Why rock a comfortable boat? The sea may be getting choppy but the storm is still over the horizon; by the time it breaks they will be in the safe haven of the pension scheme. And if a rationalization for inertia is needed it lies in the undoubted fact that changing cultures is disturbing for everyone, painful for many, and may not succeed. Thus senior management, whose presumed function is to ensure that the culture matches the business need, itself becomes the main obstacle to change.

Back in the washroom

Back in the washroom the analysis of the corporate agenda is unlikely to take place in the formal terms of culture which I have described. Although the agenda is based in the culture, it is much more detailed, and specific to a particular organization. It will be useful to take a few examples as representative of the many observations which can provide clues to the patterns which are at work. As in the case of individual patterns, the best way of predicting corporate behaviour is to assume that the future will resemble the past.

Rewards and punishments

A good way of approaching this is to see what kinds of behaviours are valued by the organization – not in terms of what is said, but in terms of what is done. A corporation has a large variety of ways in which approval or disapproval can be communicated. Some of these are obvious, such as giving promotion or withholding a salary rise. But many more are subtle – so subtle that the organization may not be conscious of using them or of the effects they have. This complex of reward and punishment is the way a corporation shapes and moulds itself; since it is a direct expression of its agenda it repays careful observation and study.

Imagine a company which declares that its primary value is service to the existing customer. This is reiterated in internal publications, in advertising, in statements to the media. You would rightly expect that the company heroes would be the customer service departments on whose meticulous and often repetitive work so much customer satisfaction depends. There would probably be regular customer surveys and other forms of structured feedback whose results would get prominence. The distribution system would have its major rewards geared to repeat sales and the establishment of long-term customers. But let's suppose that, in this particular company, the head of customer service is not treated or ranked as a key executive, and that his staff are treated as depersonalized units of work. Information about customer satisfaction is culled spasmodically and anecdotally and therefore, probably, selectively. Sales results are keyed to new business at least as clearly as to repeat business. The dramatic marketing coup is given much publicity, and the marketing executives get the rewards and the glamour. Would you not be right in thinking that this company, to paraphrase Pierpont Morgan, has two principles – one that sounds good and the real one?

I am not making a moral judgement between a business strategy which is directed at the benefit of the long-term customer and a strategy which is directed at the acquisition of new business. I am not even suggesting that pretending to do the one while really doing the other is necessarily an unsuccessful way to carry on business. My point is that it is important to know what really counts. If, in such a company, the motivation presented to support your idea is based on customer benefit when the true value held by the culture is getting new business, you will not be persuasive. If you base your motivation too nakedly on the obtaining of new business you will arouse cognitive dissonance (a technical term which, in this context, means that even hypocrisy has its limits). But if you can present an idea under the guise of customer benefit – yet which can be seen as a potential generator of new business – you may have a winning argument.

How did senior management get that way?

One may presume that, in most cases, people succeed to senior management because they have behaved in ways which accord well with the culture and the prevailing agenda. And so a useful test is to discover the previous history of the senior management of the company. Through which departments did they come on their way to the top? Were most of them long-term career people, or were they recruited at a senior level? Is there a strong emphasis on particular professional disciplines, for instance, accounting backgrounds? If there are patterns here, remember that they do not just reflect the patterns of the past; there is a probability that senior management will favour those members of middle management who are most similar to themselves.

One company had traditionally favoured chartered accountants for its chief executives. Uncharacteristically it then chose someone with marketing background. Within five years the structure of the senior management group had changed radically and it now had a heavy emphasis on marketing people. Another company was geographically

dispersed around the UK. It was noticed over a period of years that chances of promotion were directly related to where the chief executive had spent most of his service. Nor was this surprising; after all, if you want to make a promotion, you pick the people whose work you know and whom you have learnt to trust.

Successful behaviours

However, the object of this exercise is not, at least directly, to map out a path for promotion but to identify the behaviours which the organization rewards, and to use these as a guide to the patterns which prevail in the corporate agenda. They may be observed by looking at the behaviours of anyone who does well, at different levels in the organization. Are energy and forthrightness rewarded or punished? Is it better to be outspoken or reticent? What company values should you be habitually proclaiming?

The value of observation rather than merely following one's instincts is that it can help you avoid making mistakes. For instance many people assume that working hard and long hours will mark them out for reward and influence; this may be true in some companies but in others the 'workhorses' may be taken to be just that. Of course their energy is valued but they cannot be recognized as executive material since executives have time to be relaxed, mix socially in the right places, and know the right people. And it is not easy for the 'workhorse', having realized his strategic error, to change. Great reliance is placed on his activity and any reduction is resented. He may even get a reputation as a slacker among the very people who have benefited most from his previous assumption of company serfdom. Similarly, the person who conforms to every wish of his superiors, and who applauds company actions without discrimination, may get the reputation of being a faithful servant. But servant he will remain, because that is the pattern, or image, of himself he has placed in his colleagues' minds.

On the other hand, it does not follow that non-conformity will be the route to success. A fine judgement, which distinguishes between the degree of non-conformity which is seen as constructive and the degree which is seen as perverse, is required. The band may be quite narrow and its span will vary since organizations have different tolerances.

In some, a relatively high degree of non-conformity is appreciated, marking one as a person to watch. And arguably this makes for corporate success since non-conformists tend to be more intelligent, more spontaneous, more self-confident and more autonomous than conformists.[3] But this would not necessarily apply in a temple culture where the demand is to fulfil the predetermined function, and not to shake the pillars. The reaction is understandable against the background of the human instinct to avoid the unpredictable and to preserve the familiar stored patterns.

Personal characteristics

In the preface to Pygmalion, Shaw wrote: 'It is impossible for an Englishman to open his mouth without making some other Englishman despise him.' There are organizations in which an upper-class accent and good family connections can be all but essential attributes for becoming a person of significance; in others these can be a drawback, perhaps because they make colleagues whose stored patterns about different social strata are negative feel uncomfortable or at a disadvantage. There can be similar beliefs about educational standards; these may be too high or too low for a particular organization. Political views may be important; if you work in a company which has a strong right-wing bias, it may be prudent not to publicize your left-wing views. While people may tell you that your politics, within certain limits of course, are a matter of completely free choice, the suspicion remains that someone who can come to such clearly erroneous political opinions is going to be equally unsound on business decisions.

'They,' said my daughter, 'are not PLUs.' She had to explain to her ignorant parent that the initials stood for People Like Us. This reflects a strong pattern in human nature which leads to us liking more readily those who appear to have similar characteristics, values and backgrounds to our own.

Moreover, we trust people whom we see as similar, and we trust people we like. This is why there is an advantage in conforming to the general profile of the organization. Fortunately we can learn to like dissimilar people once we have become familiar with them.[4]

In a later chapter I shall say more about dress, but general appearance should be noted in this context also. In some cultures the three-piece suit would look ludicrously out of place, in others a T-shirt and jeans would be the funeral shroud of a promising career. Women whose expectation is low-grade clerical work are instantly distinguishable from the 'power dressing' of those who expect to compete for top jobs on professional terms. Length of hair and beards are details about which people have strong personal patterns. You may remember *Hair*, the musical of the 1960s in which long hair symbolized a whole movement; the strength of positive and negative reactions seems explicable only in sexual terms.

Hobbies and sports can win approval or disapproval. Time taken off to play golf may get a nod and a wink in some companies and be frowned on in others. You may race greyhounds in one company, but only horses in another. Methods of address are often traditional in an organization. Formal address throughout may be customary or only reserved for higher echelons. Many companies use first names habitually, but this may not be permitted to the 'servant' grades such as commissionaires, the canteen staff, or the chauffeur.

Stereotypes

Stereotyping (Chapter 2) can be active in business organizations, and rewards or punishments will be allotted to the appropriate stereotype. The 'workhorse' for instance may be quite capable of broad brush executive action when appropriate, but the stereotype of 'workhorse' suggests attention to detail, little sense of real priorities, willing inferiority, etc. It excludes top executive characteristics. The stereotype of long hair and jeans suggests rebelliousness and unreliability. The stereotype of the intellectual suggests inability to cope with down-to-earth practicalities. In any particular instance a stereotype judgement may be unfair; but it is understandable given that, in most cases, it is a serviceable working rule. Less rational is the persistence of stereotyping; that is, an individual who may demonstrate that he does not conform to the stereotype may still not succeed in exorcizing his initial impression – because of the tendency of patterns to self-preservation notwithstanding contrary evidence. Thus a 'workhorse' who shows himself, on occasion, to have excellent executive qualities will not necessarily find any change in his reputation subsequently.

While some stereotypes tend to be common, individual organizations will develop their own stereotypes, or variations on the common ones, from the values it wishes to preserve through its culture, or from dramatic experiences which have become part of its folk-history. One Irish company, for instance, employed an ex-priest as a salesman. He was extremely successful until the day the auditors discovered a number of irregularities in his handling of company money. He was dismissed instantly. To this day, it is almost impossible for an ex-priest to get into that organization.

Corporate values

The fly on the washroom wall, listening to the conversation and the jokes, will be able to add to his list of acceptable and unacceptable behaviour and characteristics some general principles of operation which are observed in the corporate agenda:

The power of inertia

In this company you do not seek permission to change things; that is too threatening. Instead you change things without asking, and continue until someone stops you. Usually they don't and, within a short time, your changes are accepted and established. You can even assume authority for a whole area of activity, provided there is a vacuum. After a year or two you can incorporate it in your job description without challenge.

Peace at any price

This organization cannot cope with personal conflict. No decision will be taken in favour of any idea which contradicts the wishes of another executive, unless that executive is very passive and easy-going. Doing nothing is always better than hurting people by doing something.

The open door

In this company the executives keep their doors open, no matter what the distractions may be. It is an 'open door' organization where everyone, from the highest to the lowest, can have access to everyone else. Closed doors are sinister.

One-way communication

In this company most communication goes downwards. Very little comes upwards. There are numerous facilities for staff feedback, such as consultative committees, which serve as substitutes for serious communication.

Mistakes (1)

In this company you talk a great deal about taking business risks, but you make sure that someone else is responsible – until the venture has proved successful. After that, it's a different matter.

Mistakes (2)

In this company no one is surprised if you make a mistake. In fact, if you go too long without a mistake, you may be criticized for being over-cautious.

Delay

No one turns down a new idea in this company. They merely set up a committee or ask for endless further information until the idea dies of old age.

Experiment

In this company an idea will only get through if it can be presented as an experiment. No one will ask you to monitor results. There is a rumour that the company itself was started as an experiment generations ago – and no one has yet checked to see if it succeeded.

Responding to the corporate agenda

I have suggested that it is necessary to understand the corporate agenda because individuals whom you seek to persuade will have assumed it, or aspects of it, into their personal agendas. Therefore it becomes an additional, important, dimension. But I continued by suggesting that, beyond the support of any individual, the corporation has the capacity to stifle any idea which cannot be fitted into its patterns. The principle is just the same. The methods I described in Chapters 3 and 4 for matching an idea to the patterns of the Target who is an individual can be used, with common-sense adaptations, when the Target is the company itself. Here are some examples:

- **A public relations executive wanted his company to adopt customer service as a formal value he could promote. He researched examples of good customer service, and then used these to demonstrate that he was not presenting a new idea but simply a way of benefiting from a value which was already informally present in the organization. The company was thus able to own the idea, and take responsibility for implementing what was in fact a quite radical departure.**

- **Labelling a new idea as an experiment (see the 'fly on the wall' example above) is a version of 'low-ball procedure'. The company is not frightened by the thought of an experiment and, once it has operated for a while, it is absorbed into the company's patterns.**

- **One personnel director values highly his membership of a group of personnel directors from other companies. By quoting the actions they have taken he is able to use the herd instinct to get acceptance for his ideas. When, for instance, he is criticized for salary levels he merely says: 'You know, our salary package is rather above average for companies similar to ours.' This is unanswerable.**

- **A company which plumps for safety rather than novelty will respond to a balance-of-risk approach. Once remaining unchanged is seen as more risky than undertaking change, the latter course becomes the safe one – and now fits the corporate agenda.**

Change is no easy option

I have stressed that it is hard to change a corporate culture, and therefore attempts to do this to get an idea accepted will usually fail. However, an idea which has been presented in such a way as to correspond with the agenda may, over a period of time, shape it in new directions. For instance, the acceptance of customer service as a formal value (example above) may sound harmless, but with progressive but undramatic implementation over several years, it can change the whole marketing orientation of the organization and, ultimately, its culture.

It is sometimes possible to create pockets of changed culture in areas under one's control. The objective is not to make an insulated environment, like a mystery culture, but to provide an example whose effectiveness will help others to alter their cultures, and consequent agendas, to follow suit.

A regional sales director was dissatisfied with his company's emphasis on new sales, believing that building up existing

customers for repeat sales was a better policy. When he introduced this idea into his region the time spent cultivating customers reduced his new sales, and he was put under strong pressure from his national sales manager to rescind his instructions. He resisted and, for a year or two, his stock with the company was low. But eventually his sales results overtook those of his colleagues by a large margin, and were clearly more stable. Nowadays that company has a settled policy of cultivating existing customers for which, incidentally, the national sales manager takes credit.

Senior management and change

Changing the corporate culture or its agenda may be essential for survival and prosperity yet, as I have suggested, it is almost impossible to achieve this from within the ranks. And sometimes the biggest blockage is to be found at senior management level. Nevertheless, if change is to come about, this is where it must start. Provided the chief executive and his immediate team are deeply committed to it, and are prepared to pay the price, it has a chance. They must understand the existing culture first and, having identified the factors which reinforce the existing culture, devise a plan to reduce their effect. It is crucial to pick a time when the key people at different levels are prepared to change. This is a hard judgement to make because it is easy to mistake the grumbles of criticism which are common in any organization for the real desire for change – which is much rarer. Personal example is essential. Who, for instance, believes a message that skills should be upgraded, when it is given by a management which then introduces training at one level below themselves? And they must be patient; whatever their declaration of intent, changes must be introduced gradually, and in areas which are most likely to respond well and give an example to others. Shaping rather than radical change makes it easier for new patterns to evolve; sudden changes evoke panic responses. Communication, using some of the principles of persuasion described in this book, will be essential. And communication involves, as I have said elsewhere, listening; it must be two-way.

Professor Reg Revans conducted a study into hospitals which had a high turnover of student nurses. They also had a high turnover of other staff. The only group with a low turnover was the patients, who took longer to heal than in other hospitals. Revans tracked the problem down to the nature of communications in such hospitals; these only went one way – from top to bottom. The contrasting group of hospitals, who had good staff retention and healed patients quickly, had good two-way communications and good lateral communications. The study supports the hypothesis that genuinely good communications in business keep the organization focused on shared tasks rather than the preservation of structure. It could also be an important element in enabling temple cultures to become lighter on their feet and to adapt to change without losing the inherent stability which is their strong point. Revans also maintained that the initiation and maintenance of communication flows (bad or good) was necessarily a function of senior management.[5]

So culture change is difficult. It takes great skill and a good deal of time. It may be facilitated by a new chief executive because a new man is given a period of grace and people steel themselves for some degree of change. And it is likely that his personal agenda, at the beginning of his tenure in office, will call for him to impress a new stamp. But there is a danger that his position as an 'outsider', or his introduction of preconceived ideas which do not take into account the existing culture, will bring about disaster. An existing senior management, trusted and knowledgeable, may avoid these dangers but fall foul of the problems I have already outlined. No wonder so many managements look with envy on new entrants into their market – entrants who are able to carry out the much easier task of building the right culture from scratch. Their consolation will be to realize that, in course of time, these irritating late entrants will face the same problem.

Summary

- Understanding the corporate agenda is as important as understanding the personal agenda. Indeed the personal agenda is in part formulated by the corporate agenda.

- Corporation cultures may be roughly classified as: temple, network and spider's web. The temple operates in a stable marketing environment and puts its emphasis on functions and structure rather than individuals. The network focuses on tasks and flexibility; emphasis is on teamwork and the quality of individuals. The spider's web has power, often centred in an individual, radiating from the centre. Sub-cultures may be found within the main culture, and sometimes adopt procedures to insulate themselves from change.

- Cultures tend to be self-preserving because they attract and retain people who are suited to them, and because individuals tend to adopt the values of their reference group. Corporations develop unspoken understandings (psychological contracts) with their members; these are difficult to change. Other ways of preserving culture, such as the form of pension scheme or the physical structure of the building, can be observed. Senior management may have a personal agenda which causes it to block change.

- The agenda of an organization can be better discerned from what it rewards than from what it says about itself. Clues may be provided from examining the histories of senior management, and the behaviour of those who are favoured in the company. Personal characteristics may be important. Stereotypes, some particular to that company, are likely to operate. A number of other attitudes which reveal patterns can be observed.

- Using the corporate agenda follows the same general rules as for individuals, although the techniques must be sensibly adapted. It is extremely hard to change the corporate agenda from within the ranks, but there are ways in which it may possibly be influenced.

- Although difficult, it is possible for senior management to change the corporate culture, or modify its agenda. This requires commitment, knowledge of the culture, timing, patience and excellent communication. A new chief executive may have some advantages but his ignorance of the existing culture can be a problem.

6 Projecting Personal Authority

Personal authority is not the same as real power, but it may have the same effect. The ways in which people establish their natural position in the hierarchy of a community resemble those used by species of animals, and are no doubt developed similarly. It is possible to develop greater personal authority and dominance; ways of doing this are described in this chapter. The main factors which influence whether information is believed are described.

In April 1988, Ron Chapman, a disc jockey at a Dallas radio station, asked his listeners for $20, promising nothing in return. The following day he received 4000 cheques, and the day after, 5000 cheques. When the total sum reached $240000 he had to make a further appeal imploring listeners to stop sending the money. He said: 'We're absolutely stunned. We're flabbergasted. We never promised anybody anything. That's the joy of this. We just said send the money.'[1]

Before anyone laughs too readily at the credulity of Dallas radio listeners it might be wise to reflect on the classic experiment in obedience conducted by Professor Stanley Milgram at Yale University.[2] Briefly, this experiment showed that a very high proportion of the ordinary public were willing to give innocent people electric shocks of extreme severity when they were told by someone who appeared to be in authority that it was part of a learning experiment. Significantly, groups of people who were asked independently to estimate the percentage who would comply, grossly underestimated the figure. It seems that most of us are far more prepared to accept the voice of authority than we would choose to believe. If you are confident, for instance, that you would have refused to comply with the inhuman orders given by the Nazis in Germany, you are probably fooling yourself.

In those two examples it is interesting to notice the nature of the authority involved. There is a tendency to invest well known people with authority; why else do we ask people who are famous for only being famous to give opinions on matters in which they have no special expertise? The disc jockey had no actual power, no sanctions for those who chose not to give. In the Milgram experiment the participants were volunteers who could have declined to continue at any time. But their instructors seemed to know what they were doing, and were dressed in the white coats of medical authority. The willing response in both cases was not to real power but only to the appearance and signs of power. To put it in the language of this book, the stored patterns of the responders for recognizing authority were actuated by the external signs. They assumed the substance from the appearance.

This is important for us because those who seek to persuade or to influence will often need the strength of personal authority to reinforce their case. Even if they have a measure of real power it will be weakened if they cannot project authority. And if they have no real power, which may often be the case, the ability to project authority will be essential.

Authority in our genes

It has been well documented that many species of animal, from chickens to chimpanzees, establish among themselves a hierarchy of dominance. If is often, in fact, known as the 'pecking order' from the early observations of how chickens established their rank.[3] This is a characteristic which is important for the survival of a group of animals; it ensures that the genes of the most dominant animal (who therefore mates the most) are transmitted to the next generation, and it enables order and stability to be preserved in the group.

One might expect the order of dominance to be settled by a series of bloody fights which establishes the victor. But, although this does happen under some circumstances, it is noticeable that dominance disputes are far more often decided without recourse to violence. And it has to be so because serious fighting leads to wounding and death – outcomes which would not only weaken the group but could also weaken the winner. Instead, what takes place are dominance displays, mock fights, or fights which break off before any serious damage has been done. This strategy enables two contestants to assess their chances; once they are both clear who would win and who would lose there is no point in trying to prove it through combat.

This puts an artificial emphasis on the display of strength. Male fallow deer will initially present themselves to each other sideways to show off their superior body bulk; cichlid fish will show their strength by pumping water at each other by fanning their tails; cornered gorillas will glare fiercely, beat their chests and make noisy charges – which are seldom pressed home.[4] Of course size is a good indicator of strength and therefore fighting ability, but it can be reinforced by artificial signs such as the ability of the domestic cat to fluff his fur out and make himself appear larger than he actually is. This may be accompanied by displays of willingness to fight: for example, dogs who approach each other with erect stance and head held high, followed by snarling and the showing of teeth. And so the appearance and signs of strength can become more important than strength itself, and even replace it.

Once dominance has been established the rank order can be very visible. The dog who has lost may cower, or even turn to expose his throat to demonstrate submission. Tails go down, fur goes flat. The victor may show his success by his bearing, or his nonchalance. Monkeys of different species will continuously confirm their hierarchy by rituals of dominant and submissive behaviour, one of the most familiar being the tendency of the subordinate to groom the superior, and not the other way about.[5] Dominant chimpanzees will show a relaxed courage in the face of danger; the top rooster is easy to handle and gentle on his subordinates; the bottom rooster is under strain and reacts badly to threat.[6]

'When the hunt was over there followed an extraordinary demonstration of the strong hierarchy that exists within the (wolf) pack. The alpha male (pack leader) was standing over the half-eaten carcass of the calf. As each subordinate approached it seemed to be drawn to the leader as if by a magnet. It would lower itself, pull back its ears and lips, and continue forward reluctantly as if it was being dragged against its will. The closer it got the more submissive it became.

'The alpha male, Lord of the high Arctic, had only to curl his lips and his subjects fell grovelling to the ground. The subordinates were acting like timorous pups, yet each was at least three years old and they had all just helped to attack the musk ox herd. Now, here they were, a fawning heap of insecurity, at the feet of their leader.' (from *The Company of Wolves* by Brian Jackman, Sunday Times Colour Magazine, 18 September 1988; © Times Newspapers Limited)

The need in many species to establish a social order in which each individual knows his place requires on the one hand a strong drive to obtain and maintain dominance and, on the other, a willingness to accept the reality of a submissive position and, except at the very top or very bottom, the ability to maintain both at the same time. The order will be established and preserved by systems of dominance and submission signs which achieve stability with the minimum of actual disputes.

The human pecking order

Many species of animals settle their social order in ways which differ in details but maintain a common theme. And human beings who have emerged through similar evolutionary methods, and often in similar environments, maintain the same common theme. From the scrabble for status on the social or business ladder or settling who wears the trousers within the family to the children's playground, there are winners and losers – the dominant and the submissive. Roles may change: the dominant in business may be submissive at home, the runt in the playground may be the lion of the Latin class, just as an animal may be dominant in his own territory and submissive outside it; but tendencies towards high or low dominance seem to be largely fixed by basic temperament. The modern equivalent of brute strength will always be important but, for the skilled persuader, the first subject for attention is how to project his internal authority independently of the power he may or may not possess.

Authority from the inside

Abraham Maslow, whom we have met before, carried out a number of detailed studies of men and women to establish the difference between high, low and middle dominance personalities. He was able to relate dominant behaviour to dominant feelings, and concluded that a reliable and simple way to assign people to the three categories was by asking them to describe what they felt about themselves. High dominance subjects had strong self-respect, a feeling of superiority to others in general and a confidence in their ability to handle people and situations. Low dominance personalities had general feelings of inferiority and lacked confidence in dealing with people and situations. And these characteristics tended to persist as part of the basic temperament of the individual.[7]

These studies are a little intimidating because they suggest that the die is already cast: you live in your category and there is little you can do to change it. It is not clear whether individual genes play a part in this, but it is certain that experiences do. The sense of superiority once inherited by the aristocratic classes does not require the transmission of blue blood since it can be explained by the effects of a culture which assumes itself superior and takes every opportunity to reinforce that belief amongst its young. The English public school system, ironically reserved for those with the money to pay for it, was structured in a way which gradually cultivated a sense of superiority and confidence in the young of the upper middle classes. Today these influences are less manifest, but there are plenty of others at work within the family and early associations which shape an individual's view of himself at the stage in life when the temperament is most plastic and ready to be shaped to the prevailing mould. Later experiences can modify this to some degree. A history of successful ventures, and the esteem they bring, can build self-confidence, just as the opposite may also be the case. Each of us can remember occasions when a success has brought a feeling of confidence and a failure one of depression. And this is not just in the mind: the hormones in the bloodstreams of winning and losing teams are actually different, and their behaviour changes to suit.

It is instructive to watch a top tennis match in which fortunes change more than once. It is easy to identify the disadvantaged player from his carriage and his propensity to make mistakes. But, if he recovers, his whole mien changes: he actually becomes a better tennis player under the influence of his dominance feelings. Yet the inherent skills of each player remain unchanged throughout.

Changing your dominance level

Maslow found that the level of dominance in the temperament was fixed between fairly narrow limits, but there is no doubt that worthwhile work can be done to ensure that one is at least towards the top of one's potential range. Believing that one can do this may, in itself, be a sign of dominance. One approach to this is auto-suggestion or Couéism. Émile Coué, a French doctor who died in 1926, prescribed a formula for auto-suggestion in the words (translated), 'Every day, in every way, I am getting better and better.' Couéism is no longer as wildly fashionable as it was, but the principles of his theory appear again and again in therapies which are designed to change self-image. He taught that if you repeat with sufficient frequency and sufficient conviction your belief that you possess a particular quality, your mood will gradually assume that quality and be followed by its characteristic behaviours. This may be adapted for growth of dominance in a number of ways:

- Keep in the forefront of your mind any successes you may have had; push any failures into the background. If you have any recorded evidence of success, say, a note or a certificate marking an achievement, keep it by you.

- Encourage yourself to fantasize about being successful. My favourite fantasy is giving my first press interview after being elected Pope. In particular, see yourself actually being successful at the enterprise you are about to undertake. This will be greatly helped by careful preparation. The well prepared salesperson, for instance, finds it actually hard to believe that his prospective customer will not buy.

- Make a list of your good qualities, disciplining yourself to omit any qualifications or faults. Study this list, look at it often, remember it.

- Repeat to yourself, often and convincingly, your version of Coué's formula; it might be: 'I feel confident, I feel in control, I'm in charge.'

Using your dominance display

The approach I have described concentrates on getting your mind right, knowing that appropriate actions will follow. A second approach is complementary: getting your actions right, knowing that your mind will follow. Just pause in your reading for a moment and try the following experiment. Stand up straight, in a military position with chest out and chin up. Then say: 'I am a louse, I am a failure, everyone looks down on me, I'm second rate.' Try it now.

It's a strange feeling, isn't it? The words and the stance don't go together. You could never convince anyone listening to you that you really were a louse; you certainly couldn't convince yourself.

Developing your dominance display requires thinking about some of the ways in which dominance is physically signalled – the ways which promote a feeling of dominance in ourselves and present a pattern to others which they recognize as dominance. The whole range of the display is extensive and subtle, but I shall concentrate on the main factors.

The human dominance display

In animals, size can be an important factor in dominance. In human beings the effects are more complex, presumably because we can more easily recognize that strength does not always go with size since we are aware of many strengths beyond the physical. Nevertheless there is some correlation and many, but by no means all, studies have shown that the leaders in a group tend to be taller than their rank and file. This is reflected in our vocabulary when we speak of someone as being a 'big man' and of others as the 'little guys'. I recall my mother speaking of her lawyer as her 'little man', when she barely reached five foot and he was well over six. We also tend to impute size to the powerful as when it was said of Charlemagne that he was eight foot tall, could eat a fat goose at a sitting and could lift a knight in full armour off the ground.

An actor was introduced to several audiences in Australia, sometimes as a professor from Cambridge, sometimes as a lecturer and sometimes as a graduate. When the audiences were afterwards asked to estimate his height they judged the 'professor' to be tallest, and the 'graduate' to be shortest.[8]

So when (English) policemen wear conical helmets, bishops wear mitres and tribal chieftains wear elaborate headdresses they make use of the primitive stored pattern of height to reinforce their authority.

However, and perhaps fortunately for those of average height, that is not the end of the story. Napoleon, Nelson, and Viscount Montgomery were all short men yet they were renowned for their dominance qualities. More important than actual height is carriage. The experiment I asked you to try a few lines back relied on the fact that people who have an upright carriage – to which the nearest approximation is the military stance – convey dominance both to themselves and others. They exude confidence and control and they convey the impression that they are important; whereas even the tallest person who walks with bowed back and a down-turned glance conveys deference and submissiveness. It is no coincidence that soldiers are drilled into an upright posture just as we may encourage our children to stand up straight.

Developing an upright carriage is not a difficult habit to acquire; it is even possible, through habit, to sustain it when we happen to be at a disadvantage. And since it can be imitated so easily it can be assumed by those who actually lack the corresponding qualities. But there is another characteristic which, although it can be developed, is very hard for someone without a measure of dominance to acquire.

Relaxacat

We once had a half Siamese cat named Misky. He moved around the house, which he clearly owned, in a slow, relaxed way – lording it over the others. He had established several dozing places, where the sunshine or the heat of the boiler warmed him. If another cat took one of his places he was not angry; he simply went and stood nearby; and his spot was vacated without delay. Occasionally a kitten would come and annoy him; he stood it patiently for a few minutes, then he raised a large paw and, with a lazy cuff, scudded the kitten across the room. His enemies in the garden were another matter. He would lie in wait, apparently relaxing in the sun, until the right moment came. Then this slow moving creature would hurl himself forward like a shell from a gun, reaching maximum velocity instantaneously. His legs were so blurred that he gave the impression of travelling a foot off the ground, and the pain of the impact as he hit his enemy amidships was felt by any onlooker as a thud in the stomach.

No wonder cats are so admired, and so feared. They epitomize dominance. The characteristic of relaxation is a crucial dominance trait; it can belong only to those who are completely confident that they are in control of the situation, that they can deal with any emergency without difficulty. They may not, in fact, move particularly slowly but the ease of their movement gives that impression. They are not thrown by the little nuisances of life, which they can afford to ignore. But when they need to move fast they are decisive, and sometimes awe-inspiring in the execution.

By contrast low dominance people are likely to live under tension. Their movements are jerky and fidgety; they react quickly to nuisance, and with irritation to any slight at the position they believe they are entitled to hold. Their actions are tentative and often ineffective. The environment controls them, and they must continually be on their guard.

The signs of relaxation and the signs of tension are very obvious to the observer; they are dealt with at length in books on non-verbal communication (see Bibliography). But it is interesting to notice one's own reactions. Do you get flustered in an emergency or do you simply focus your efforts on dealing with it as effectively as possible? Are you very conscious of what people think of you and how they react to you, or do you take a good reaction for granted, maybe because you do not really care? Do you treat people with the same good manners that Misky observed because you can afford to do so, or must you be constantly insisting on your rights?

I have said that this characteristic of relaxation is hard to simulate; it is almost impossible to look relaxed unless you are relaxed. But fortunately it is possible for most people to learn how to relax, and to make it a way of life which increases their sense of control over situations, which will in turn be expressed in the way they behave. There are several good books on the subject (see Bibliography) and therapists available for those who need a helper at the initial stages. Mastering the art of relaxation brings many benefits beyond improving one's dominance level and the presentation of oneself as a high dominance person.

Gaze

In a troop of monkeys and in a troop of human beings, subordinates spend much time looking at the most important person. He is the leader they must be ready to follow; his are the decisions to which they must immediately respond. Yet gaze can also be a characteristic of high dominance, though used in quite a different way. The leader, for all his insouciance, must be aware of his environment so that he can lead others to safety; he is monarch of all he surveys, and so he surveys it all. He will look about him steadily, holding his gaze, while lesser people break off and look away. He does not stare unless, and this is very rare, he needs to threaten; he looks because he chooses to.

This steady direct look, which is neither a threat nor a gesture of intimacy, is often used by a dominant person at the beginning of a social encounter; and this may be the main reason why the relative level of two people is established at their first meeting, and is hard to change afterwards.

A good way of experiencing high dominance gaze is to observe yourself while driving a motor car. Your carriage is upright to ensure good vision, and your eyes are continually surveying the environment so as to respond to it effectively. The good driver is relaxed and neat in his movements but at moments of sudden danger he takes instinctive, lightning action. Aggressive drivers are, of course, signalling that the temporary, artificial dominance provided by the motor car is not their natural condition; their subordinate temperament cannot cope easily with threats.

Defining the social situation

A young friend of mine, David O'Hanlon, travelled on his own to the USSR. At the border he was stopped and subjected to a long interview about his political opinions. He was asked which newspapers he read, and then challenged with the question: 'Why do you not read the (Communist) *Morning Star*? He replied: 'Because I don't like their sports page.' The interview terminated quickly, and he was allowed to enter.

It is a trait of dominance to define the social situation. The tone, the atmosphere, the work that will be done are decided, often unconsciously, by the dominant person; he does not fit into the setting, the setting is formed around him. Usually this is effected by the dominant person speaking first, or being the first to give direction to what is happening. This is another instance of the primacy effect, and is often powerful enough to allow the dominant person to maintain his pre-eminence thereafter by the occasional shaping remark – leaving the chattering sparrows to do most of the talking, under the ranging eye of the hawk.

But social situations do not always arise in such a formalized way. Have you ever stalled your motor car and found yourself getting increasingly flustered as you sense, or hear, the irritation of the drivers held up behind you? If so, take a leaf from the lady in the cartoon (I cannot recall the source) who went to the man in the car behind and said: 'Why don't you start my car, while I toot your horn?' That's worth remembering the next time you find other people defining the social situation for you.

My favourite story of continuing to define the social situation under unusually difficult circumstances concerns a kinsman of mine who was sentenced (for the most honourable of reasons) to be executed by a firing squad. He shook hands with the members of the squad and, unblindfolded, gave them the order to fire. I suspect that, even in front of the dead body, his executioners continued to feel at something of a disadvantage.[9]

Dress

Uniforms and badges of rank are examples where dress is commonly used to define an authority role. A less obvious, but very effective example – as Professor Milgram's experiment showed – is the white coat with its medical overtones and, at the other end of the spectrum, the black garb of the cleric. Both are favoured by fraudsters who know they can rely on others taking them at face value. Choices are more difficult in ordinary business situations since cultures vary, and so do fashions. Once again, it is necessary to observe what the most successful people wear. This is not a question of slavish imitation but an acceptance that within that particular community a certain style of dress is recognized through habitual patterns as belonging to people of consequence. You may feel confident enough to go against the trend, and, if you pull it off, you are certainly making a high dominance gesture. But there is a risk.

Formal distinctions in dress as a mark of rank are as old as civilization, and occur in cultures as varied as ancient Egypt and the Aztecs. In medieval Europe 'sumptuary' laws defining dress according to station in life were passed. Christine de Pisan, the earliest professional woman writer in Europe, firmly castigated the wives of merchants for dressing like their betters. (*Le Livre du Trésor de la Cité des Dames*, 1405)

Remember also that the right clothes for you help you to feel good. Many people take the trouble to dress particularly carefully when they know they have a challenging day ahead – not because they expect others to notice, but because they know it gives them a confidence which will show in their bearing.

For a number of years I attended marriage counselling residential conferences, invariably wearing an old jumper and baggy corduroys. But on one occasion when I was held late at the office I arrived in a three-piece suit with the usual trimmings. This came as a shock to my counselling colleagues who had always assumed that I taught at a university; it took them some time to adjust to the possibility that I might be a business person. Although they were well trained in avoiding easy assumptions and knew me quite well, they were unable to avoid classifying me according to my 'uniform'.

The power of the well tailored business suit to command authority was demonstrated in a study where the experimenter crossed the street, illegally and against the lights. When he was wearing a business suit his lead was followed by 3½ times as many other jaywalkers as when he was wearing casual clothes. This experiment took place in Texas where, for all I know, the frequency of well tailored business suits is different from, say, the City of London.[10]

Accent

Professor John Honey in his *Does Accent Matter?* (see Bibliography) reports that several studies demonstrate that 'received pronunciation' – that is, the accent of the usual BBC newsreader, and shared by about three per cent of the population – carries the highest prestige. The owner is rated as more intelligent, competent and having higher leadership qualities than those with other accents; among women, the owner is also rated more highly in strength, initiative and femininity. This stress on using the accent of the ruling classes (centred in London and the South East) dates, he tells us, at least from Shakespeare's time and was an important factor in the growth of boarding schools which, until recently, could be expected to refine the accents of their pupils. Nor is this confined to England. In the United States the presence of non-standard forms of speech, suggesting lack of education, can be damaging; in Quebec the accent and usages of Parisian French are admired in preference to Canadian French.

This does not conflict with my remark in Chapter 5 that an 'upper-class accent . . . can be a drawback' in certain organizations. Where a social grouping marks its identity at least to some degree by a shared working class or local accent, received pronunciation may be seen as exaggerated and effeminate. This effect can be tested, if you are sceptical, by becoming a Yorkshire coalminer and continuing to use received pronunciation.

A close friend of mine did his compulsory military service in the ranks. When he emerged I noticed immediately that his former, rather marked, received pronunciation had flattened considerably. He told me that this had made life much more comfortable for him. Shortly afterwards he became an underwriting member at Lloyds, at that time an

enclave of the upper middle classes, and his original accent restored itself virtually overnight.

It becomes increasingly difficult to develop received pronunciation after the early teens. But many people are successful in doing so, as a result of continuously mixing with received pronunciation speakers or having elocution training. Perhaps the outstanding modern example is Mrs Thatcher whose current use of received pronunciation is masterly. Only natural received pronunciation speakers can detect the difference and they, as I have said, only represent 3 per cent of the population.

Whose problem is it?

If you have a subordinate who fails to come up to scratch and, after due thought and consideration for his welfare, you decide to sack him or her, whose problem is it? If the computer department purchases expensive equipment for you which doesn't match your specifications, whose problem is it? If an advertising agency has gone to a great deal of trouble and cost to make a presentation to get your account, and you turn them down, whose problem is it?

At the intellectual level we can see that it is the subordinate, the computer department and the agency who have the problem. But at the emotional level it may be different. Most of us seek to please, and to avoid hurting other people (although this often turns out to be a way of avoiding hurt to ourselves – not charity but self-indulgence). The dominant person is concerned first and foremost with achieving the task he has in hand; he does not shy away from allowing people to be hurt if that is a necessary outcome of the situation. He distinguishes between *his* problems, for which he takes responsibility, and the problems of other people, which he leaves *them* to shoulder.

It is worth reflecting on how much anxiety and inefficiency in business (and daily) life arises from taking on other people's problems, either emotionally or actually. Willingness to do so is a low-dominance trait.

Aggressive dominance

If leadership dominance is characterized by upright stance, aggressive dominance is characterized by the crouch of someone who is ready to spring. We all know people who live on a short fuse; one step too far and a burst of temper explodes. One senses fierce emotions seething just below the surface like a touchy volcano. Such people undoubtedly wield power; it is based on the fear of triggering an unpleasant emotional confrontation, often reinforced by such real sanctions as the person may control.

Aggressive dominance bears a superficial similarity to leadership dominance. For example, aggressively dominant people will often define the social situation – since it is less painful to allow this than to risk the alternative. They will often define the emotional atmosphere since their tension pervades. But the source is quite different. Aggressive dominance arises from exaggerated fears of loss of control; it is based on weakness rather than strength, and rules by fear rather than by respect.

Aggressive dominance is also used as a form of management control and may be effective in certain leadership situations, at least for a period of time. But its effects are essentially unstable since subordinates will seek to escape wherever possible and, in the meanwhile, will concentrate on avoiding the eruption rather than contributing their best.[11]

Credibility

The question of credibility arises in one form or another throughout this book. People tend to believe what they want to believe; that is, whatever reinforces their existing patterns or is consistent with them. But, beyond this, there are some common patterns specifically related to credibility – some conditions which, when measured by experiment, appear to affect the believability of a message, assuming that other circumstances are equal.[12]

- The projection of personal authority is reinforced if the communicator is believed to have an expertise which is relevant to the message.

- A source of credibility, reported by Professor Honey (see above), which may have similar origins, is the use of received pronunciation – and, doubtless, its equivalent in other countries – because it suggests education and competence.

- If the communicator is seen as someone who has inaccurate or biased information, his credibility will be low, although the listener's judgement of bias may well be affected by whether or not the message is welcome:

A firm of consultants produced a recommendation which ran counter to the prejudices of the board of directors. Since it was largely based on interviews with employees it was supposed that the interviewees had taken the opportunity to get all their grumbles off their chests, anonymously and to outsiders. Since the recommendation was based on such contaminated sources it could safely be ignored.

- A factor in credibility is the suspicion of reporting bias. The phrase: 'He would, wouldn't he?' said by Mandy Rice-Davies in the Profumo scandal of 1963 has passed into the English language. It epitomizes the assumption that people see, and therefore report, reality in the way which suits their interests. It is harder to carry conviction when acceptance of the message is seen as favourable to the communicator. It is a good plan to present a proposal in such a way that one's personal benefit is played down; it may even be possible to hint that its acceptance will actually be disadvantageous to you. An alternative approach is to emphasize that one realizes that acceptance of the proposal will be personally beneficial, but nevertheless the case is being made on objective grounds. The highlighting of the listener's potential prejudice will make it difficult to sustain.

- In Chapter 1 the salesman made positive use of a limitation of his product (low, early surrender values) by emphasizing it, and thereby reinforcing his trustworthiness. The voluntary introduction of points which detract from the presenter's case – but are not strong enough to destroy it – can enhance credibility.[13]

Thames Television was strongly criticized by the Government for broadcasting a programme, *Death on the Rock*, which was about the killing of IRA members in Gibraltar. The Government argued that it could prejudice the forthcoming inquest. In January 1989 the Windlesham Report was published, and substantially exonerated Thames. It was an independent report, but commissioned by Thames. In the controversy which followed the fact that the authors had criticized Thames for some relatively minor aspects of its conduct was often quoted as evidence of the objectivity of the report. Thames's sportsmanlike acceptance of these criticisms was taken as a sign of its sincerity.

- I have noted, in Chapter 5, that similarity to the listener tends to aid credibility; the attractiveness of the communicator is also a factor. In the 1960 US presidential election the greater attractiveness of John Kennedy as he appeared in televised debates was thought to have influenced the outcome in his favour over Richard Nixon. Nixon was more successful than Kennedy in radio debates. Attractive students soliciting signatures for a petition were significantly more successful than the less attractive. In one study of 74 people on trial for criminal offences, those previously rated as physically attractive proved twice as likely to avoid prison as the less attractive. Similarly, in staged trials for negligence, personal attractiveness earned the complainant nearly twice the damages awarded to the less well favoured.[14]

Summary

- There is an innate pattern which recognizes the signs and symbols of authority; people often accept such authority without question, and are ready to give surprising degrees of obedience.

- Many species of animals develop a 'pecking order' which is usually established without fighting, thus putting an emphasis on the display of strength rather than the use of it. The hierarchy will be preserved and confirmed by rituals of dominance and submission.

- There are many parallels with the human 'pecking order', although what counts as strength, or substantial power, is more varied. It is valuable to study the display of dominance, either to reinforce substantial power or as a substitute for it.

- Although the circumstances in which one is dominant may vary, Maslow established that levels of dominance were a reflection of temperament – and best measured by an individual's feelings about himself. However, one way of maximizing potential dominance is through auto-suggestion.

- Another approach is to use the physical signals of dominance and thus cultivate the complementary feelings. Stance, relaxation, gaze, defining the social situation, dress and accent, and deciding whose problem it is, are factors; these can be studied more fully in specialist books.

- Aggressive dominance may be mistaken for leadership dominance since some of its effects are similar. But its source is in weakness rather than strength, and it inhibits good work rather than promoting it.

- Some factors which increase credibility are: apparent expertise, accent, objectivity, similarity, and attractiveness. Suspicion that the communicator is badly informed or biased, or will gain personal advantage from being believed, are negative factors.

7 Winning and Using Supporters

The skilful cultivation of allies and friends in support of an idea is an effective use of the herd instinct – that primitive pattern which tells us that there is safety in numbers. Lobbying has an important place in the armoury of anyone who wants to get his own way in business. Allies need to be selected carefully and used with discretion. You must decide how they are going to be used and whether you will enlist them by direct or indirect means. Beyond the methods described generally in this book there are certain patterns which are particularly effective for this.

The life assurance salesman uses lobbying, or employs witnesses to give him credibility, in a variety of ways. At one time I was doing business among television actors. With their permission, I was able to quote the names of many actors who were already clients of mine. After only a few names had been casually mentioned my new customer would indicate some degree of resentment that I had seen so many (inferior?) actors before finally getting around to him. Some salesmen will ask satisfied clients to write a few lines of approbation on their headed notepaper, or will invite the prospective customer to telephone a client known to them both.

Many new ideas, particularly if they are radical, require the support of a number of people before they become acceptable, and the credibility of a message is greatly reinforced by independent views. In Chapter 4 I used the example of Sheila Robinson who had to be persuaded that heavy new expenditure on advertising would pay off in business results. The proposal involved risk, and there was no way of demonstrating certain success. An element in the persuader's strategy was to quote examples of other successful companies which had taken similar steps. But the case would have been much strengthened if some of Sheila's colleagues, particularly those whose opinions she valued, were seen as being in support. Their views would have been taken as evidence that the idea was soundly based, and she would have been comforted by knowing that she would not have to fight opposition within her own organization. The loneliness which afflicts every leader who takes on a new direction would have been, to some extent, allayed.

Building your lobbying base

Having a reputation among colleagues for cooperation, friendliness, knowledge and personal authority is valuable for its own sake. But it is also important for lobbying. If you suddenly find that you need allies for your cause, it is too late to develop these relationships from scratch, and your motives will be deservedly suspect. But cultivate potential allies before you need them, and they will be ready to hand when the moment arrives.

In building up good relationships around the office you will get to know a great deal about how your colleagues think and what values they have. You will probably know them better than you will know your boss because the exchange of information is likely to be less inhibited. The intimate knowledge which you obtain of their stored patterns will be useful when you want to enlist their support.

Key allies

Not all your colleagues will be equally useful. You have to identify those who are well respected, with views which carry weight. You may remember the example in Chapter 3 of the finance director on whose judgement the boss placed great reliance. He would be an important ally. Look for the people who carry power; often this will be resource power. If your idea involves computer systems, the head of this area should be on your side – at the least, you can't afford to have him against you. If there are tricky legal questions to be handled your relationships with the law department may be important. Remember those people whose work is closely aligned with predominant company values; if the sales force is king you may need the sales director; if product quality is king you may need the product director.

Be aware of how your potential allies influence each other. If the personnel chief habitually agrees with the sales director you may be able to use this to secure two allies at once. If they habitually disagree you will have to use other tactics. And most organizations will contain negative allies, that is, people whose support is taken to be evidence that the idea is unsound. Often such a view is wholly or largely unjustified; groups seem to need a scapegoat – someone on whom can be conveniently projected many of the follies from which the rest hope they are free. Scapegoats are often survivors because the group needs them, and they are eager to give support to relieve their own isolation. High dominance people, who do not share the group's psychological need, will often champion scapegoats. But, as allies, scapegoats should be avoided.

Using potential allies

You may want to use your allies by quoting their support for your proposals at the time they are being made; or you may want them to speak for themselves if your proposal is being discussed in committee; or you may simply want them to be primed because it is likely that the Target will consult them while considering your idea.

Quoting allies as part of your presentation needs subtlety. If you simply say: 'Tom and Margaret and Fred and Bill all think this is a first rate idea,' you run the risk of making Sheila feel that you are ganging up on her. Ganging up means pressure, and pressure means loss of control. Nor is it enough to report a simple recommendation – some substance and detail must be given.

The quality of the ally is the key and, in this instance, you may want to use only Margaret, who is the finance director, and Fred, who has a reputation for caution. The others may be useful later. Introduce your witnesses obliquely, and put some flesh on the bones of their support. For example, you might say:

> **'I thought I'd better run through the figures with Margaret just to check our cash-flow position. She says she doesn't think there's any real problem, but it might be better for tax reasons to borrow the money rather than take it straight out of capital. She said she might argue a bit about the discounting periods I've chosen, though. Actually she came up with some good ideas about advertising messages, and I'm hoping to talk to her a bit more about that.'**

In a few seconds you have communicated that Margaret has thought about the finances of the proposition and, almost incidentally, that she is favourably disposed towards the idea. You may like to work out for yourself the reason for inserting her reservations about the discounting periods.

Getting support from allies in committee is also a question of quality rather than quantity. But with one or two key people on your side the rest are likely to follow. They do not always have to know that they're on your side (see below); and this will help you to avoid giving the impression of orchestration. Beware of the false ally who will not support in public the views he has given in private. And beware the weathervanes who turn the way the boss is blowing.

Enlisting support

You will be using the principles and techniques of persuasion, described generally in this book, to enlist the support of your colleagues for your cause, bearing in mind the individual patterns to which they will be likely to respond. But you must decide whether you are explicitly asking for support or just sowing the seeds which will be harvested when your allies' opinion is sought by the Target. The former gives you more certainty since you will know the strength you comand in advance; the latter is more hazardous because only the outcome will tell you whether your seeds have taken healthy root. The method may be decided by what you know of your potential ally; if he is the sort of person who would be unlikely to undertake support at your explicit request you will use the indirect method. And you may prefer this in any event because the support which is given will be voluntary and spontaneous – and therefore convincing.

Indirect approaches

A most effective method of getting indirect support is to ask for help in the preparation of your idea:

> **'Margaret, I'm putting some new advertising ideas up to Sheila. I wonder if you could give me five minutes to go through the figures I've prepared. They're only rough at the moment, and you might be able to show me how to set them out in a way that makes them really clear. It would help me a lot if you could.'**

Notice the two important patterns at work. The first is that people love to be able to give help. As Nathaniel Hawthorne said in *The Scarlet Letter* (1850), 'It is to the credit of human nature, that, except where its selfishness is brought into play, it loves more readily than it hates.' Margaret has nothing to lose by helping you, and she has a comforting sense of self-esteem to gain by doing you a favour.

> **Some years ago I broke my leg; eventually I was able to use public transport – wearing a half-plaster and using two sticks. Taxi drivers helped me, friendly hands lifted me on to bus platforms, my colleagues held up traffic so I could cross the road. I was conscious of conferring a real benefit on my fellow creatures by giving them an opportunity to help me at very little cost to themselves.**

The second pattern is one we have encountered before: if a person participates in an idea, even in a minor way, he assumes a degree of ownership of the idea. The salesman in Chapter 1 made sure that, wherever possible, it was the prospective customer who came to the conclusion rather than him. Some salesmen will get the customer to write down the figures or feed them into his lap-top computer in order to reinforce the sense of teamwork and commitment. The recording studio, in Chapter 3, used the Eiffel Tower slide so that their clients would assume ownership by excluding this. Similarly, if Margaret has helped to prepare the figures she is likely to have become, if only to a small degree initially, a sponsor of the idea. The foot-in-the-door effect (Chapter 3) will then take over.

The other ally you had in mind to use was Fred; since he has a reputation for caution he will be valuable because allies who appear to be going against their natural inclinations give a strong boost to credibility (Chapter 6). You might use the same principle but apply it in a way which is appropriate to him:

'Fred, I've got an idea I want to show to Sheila. I wonder whether I could run through it with you. There are one or two aspects she might not like at first sight, and you're just the sort of person who could suggest some ways I could put it across.'

You may notice that, in addition to the flattery involved in seeking his opinion, you are implying that Fred is someone who has some skills in putting over new ideas. We often assume that people are flattered primarily by references to their known good qualities. But in fact they are much more complimented by references to the qualities they feel they have but which are seldom recognized.

A marriage counsellor friend of mine is an efficient organizer. She also has a very kind heart. But she suspects that many people notice only her competence – indeed they often congratulate her on it. She told me that she would cheerfully exchange every compliment she receives for her

good organization (of which she is perfectly well aware) for one remark acknowledging the kindness of her heart. You may like to test this for yourself by thinking of the qualities you have which usually go unnoticed; ask yourself whether a compliment about these has a special value to you.

In addition to deliberately planned occasions for enlisting allies indirectly you should take opportunities for testing the broad opinions of your colleagues by informal conversations which, perhaps, do not present your ideas as a whole but are sufficiently close to enable you to gauge views. You might, for instance, discuss in a general way the value of advertising to the company. And this will quickly give you a sense of the prevailing feeling. Such conversations will tell you many things. If you find that most opinions are against you, you will have to reassess the situation. Is your Target easily swayed by general opposition or is he inclined to take it as a challenge? Are those who hold contrary opinions people of influence – or are they negative allies (in which case their opposition may be useful)? Will you need more propaganda at this level before it will be wise to present the idea? If, on the other hand, you find supporting opinion you must decide how best to use it. You might take no action, and just rely on these positive opinions emerging informally. You may be able to identify the potential allies who can be used in the ways I have already discussed. And this may require you, in successive conversations, to focus more sharply on the idea you have in mind. With care it may well be that you have an ally who is convinced that he was responsible for the idea in the first place.

Whenever I launched a new product I would take care to acknowledge the work which had been done by various people in its preparation. Invariably I would then be contacted by three or four more people who felt that I should have mentioned that they were responsible for the concept in the first place. But, as I have said, the person who seeks to get his own way in business must be satisfied with doing just that. The price will often be that others take the credit.

Direct approaches

A direct request for support may contain the danger of appearing to force the issue, or produce the appearance of an orchestrated campaign. But there are many occasions when explicit support from key people will be valuable. And often it is possible to avoid the dangers of putting the Target under pressure by clarifying the situation before suspicions are aroused:

> **'Frankly, Sheila, I recognized that the financial aspects of this idea would be the key ones you would want to examine first. So I've had a long discussion with Margaret to satisfy myself that it all hangs together. And she tells me that she's fully behind it, though naturally she's eager to discuss it with you personally because she knows you like to make up your own mind on these things.'**

I have suggested that you should only canvass direct support from those who, you know from experience, are prepared to give it. Your informal conversations will have helped you to identify sympathizers, and you will be able to use their own views in cementing their commitment. Once again, a direct request for assistance will be most effective:

> **'Fred, I've been thinking about those chats we had on the company's advertising, particularly the remarks you made about the need for us to have a high profile should the market turn against us. I've been turning it over in my mind and I've come up with a plan which I want to show Sheila. But you know what Sheila's like – she never makes a move unless she feels you're happy about it. I'm really after your support because without it I won't get to first base. Let me run through the plan with you; I think you'll find it's pretty close to the ideas we discussed – see if you agree.**

Of course, you'll be delighted if Fred suggests some modifications which you can incorporate.

Enlisting the boss's boss

On the whole, don't. For most people nothing is more infuriating than to discover that their power of decision has been removed by *force majeure*. Even if they are obliged to accede they are still in a strong enough position to dilute the idea or to use negative power to ensure that it fails or never materializes. Remember the reactance pattern (Chapter 3) where the instinctive response to loss of control is irrational and destructive. Just occasionally the Target, having low dominance, may be so malleable to higher authority that such a tactic would work, but who wants a boss like that anyway?

But in those companies where relationships are informal, and direct contact with senior levels of the hierarchy is usual, some benefit may be gained, provided the matter is handled with care. The ideal situation occurs when the boss's boss happens in conversation to express an opinion which supports or complements your idea. Build on this through your wide-eyed interest in his perspicacity, and thus confirm his commitment. More often you will need to raise the subject yourself – but in a very informal and conversational way since he should never know you are enlisting his support to use with your Target.

You may never need to mention this senior support to your Target, knowing that he will discuss your idea with his boss in due course. But, should you mention it, never suggest that the Target's freedom of action is curtailed. This would be a better way:

> **'Yes, I see what you mean, Sheila. Even if you agree the idea is right for us, everything will depend on selling it upstairs. Still, that might not be impossible. When Mr Hunter popped down the other day to borrow some photos I had on file, he made some remark about us getting better known as a company. It could be that there would be something for you to build on there.'**

The implied context of that remark is that the reference to Hunter is not invoked to persuade Sheila of the value of the idea – as far as you're concerned, that's her decision – but to give Sheila some encouragement that she can sell the idea. Only incidentally does the message that Hunter is a supporter come across.

Loyalty to your allies

Be very careful not to exaggerate the support your allies are willing to give you. Apart from the simple matter of honesty, you will need your allies again and again over the years. Once get a reputation for taking names in vain, and you will find yourself friendless. Nor is there any need. Provided that an ally is in general favour of your idea, expressing any reservations he may have can only lend credibility to his witness.

Be sparing in your cultivation of allies – both the numbers you use, and the occasions for which you employ them. If you are seen to collect a lobby too often, you may build up a resistance to your methods which makes them counter-productive. Select the key occasions; and use other methods for the less important ideas.

Although it may never be made explicit, lobbying involves an element of bargaining. You must be ready to repay your allies by supporting their ideas when they need it. But a knowledge of the lobbying process will at least enable you to be aware of what they are after.

Summary

- Lobbying, or the enlisting of allies, uses the herd instinct to gain credibility and strengthen your case.

- Build up your lobbying base by maintaining good relationships and the respect of your colleagues. This will also give you a knowledge of their stored patterns which you can use to cultivate their support.

- Pick allies with discrimination – people who have influence or resource power. Be aware of how allies influence each other. Avoid negative allies.

- You may want to quote the support of an ally as part of your presentation, or you may need allies' support in committee, or they may be passive allies whom the Target is likely to consult. Be very selective about allies you quote to avoid the Target feeling cornered. Quality is more important than numbers in committee, too. Beware the turncoat ally.

- You may enlist support indirectly, and your best method may be to ask for help with some aspect of the idea. Remember that being asked to help builds self-esteem, and that assistance gives ownership. Informal conversations with colleagues may help you to identify potential allies who can then be cultivated.

- Some allies may be asked directly to give support, and you can avoid giving the Target an impression of an organized campaign by stating that you have obtained support, and why.

- Getting the Target's boss on your side will be counter-productive if the Target feels loss of control as a result. But, if the boss's boss has become an ally through indirect means, this may be useful provided great care is taken.

- Be loyal to your allies; report them correctly. Don't devalue the currency by lobbying on unimportant matters. Remember that giving support is giving a favour; be ready to reciprocate.

8 Supercharging Staff Performance

The secret of getting superior performance out of staff lies in developing staff who genuinely believe they are capable of it. Fortunately the manager has a number of ways available which he can use to give his people a high self-image. But he has to know how and when to use them.

Some years ago I became temporary assistant manager of a branch office. In my former branch I had accumulated a massive amount of paper – reports, statistics, correspondence – which might come in useful one day. I threw them all away, and so my new office was unnaturally tidy. I knew it would not be for long. Then one day a member of the branch remarked to me on how well organized my office looked. I beamed. But I was caught; for the remainder of my time in that branch I took care to maintain my reputation for orderliness. What had happened? I had seen an image of myself as a tidy person reflected in the opinion of a colleague. I liked the image; I lived up to it.

Self-image and performance

The manager who knows how to build a high self-image in his staff will be capable of supercharging their performance. Under his hands quite ordinary people will extend their capacity beyond limits which anyone, except the manager, ever thought possible. Sticks and carrots may bring about small improvements but when someone has a high self-image he will really fly.

Frank Smith, thought by many to be the best branch manager Sun Life of Canada has ever had, believed in building a high image in his salesmen. He knew there was no target beyond them. Today, in retirement, he has the satisfaction of seeing that, out of the eight most senior executives in the UK, three are former members of his branch – one of them the chief executive.

People live up to the images they have of themselves – bad or good. The executive who sees himself as a creative person tends to behave in that way; the person who sees himself as a hard worker, works hard; the person who believes he has little to contribute, contributes little. And the manager who can create high self-image will create high performance.

The building of self-image

Throughout life human beings build up their self-images. The process starts in the first few years where the infant receives from its parents a basic picture of itself (perhaps as a 'lovable' person, or perhaps as a 'naughty, unacceptable' person). These basic views of self, which are quite hard to change later, are gradually filled out by new experiences, become more complex, and continue to evolve – although at a slower rate and in more trivial ways. We may even have sub self-images which vary according to different situations – thus the tough top businessman, the irritable husband, the kindly bumbling grandpa may all be one and the same person presenting different aspects of his image in response to different situations.[1]

A mixture of influences creates self-image. Heredity and early upbringing are fundamental (the balance between the two is disputed by psychologists); experience of one's own successes or failures also makes an important contribution. Another powerful factor – particularly relevant to this chapter – is external influence: the way in which a self-image is formed through the reaction of other people. They act to us like mirrors; and in their responses we see a reflection of ourselves which tells us what we are. And because we then start to behave in accordance with this, the image is self-reinforcing. When interviewers, specially trained for the purpose, used 'friendly' and 'unfriendly' approaches to candidates, the candidates reacted in accordance with the treatment received. Independent judges viewing videotapes of the interviews rated those who had received the 'unfriendly' treatment as significantly less able candidates. They had lived up (or lived down?) to the image the interviewer had given them.[2]

Most people can check this for themselves. Are there some people in your life who think highly of you and make you feel good? How do you behave when you're with those people? Are there some who have a negative view of you and in whose presence you always seem to say the wrong thing or behave clumsily? Do you know any married people who have a poor opinion of their partners, and is that opinion helpful or damaging?

The effects of self-image

This response to the expectations of others has been recorded in many contexts, such as the 'friendly' and 'unfriendly' interviewing techniques described above, and in educational situations.

A typical experiment to investigate this would be: a teacher is given a new class, and is told that the bright children are seated on the right and the less bright on the left; in fact the children are seated randomly. When the class is given tests the children on the right tend to get significantly better marks. It appears that the teacher attends more to the 'bright' children, invites them to contribute more frequently and in other subtle ways communicates a good opinion of their capacities.[3]

J. Sterling Livingston, former Professor of Business Administration at Harvard Business School, sums up its application to business situations in these words:

'I have documented this phenomenon in a number of case studies prepared during the past decade for major industrial concerns. These cases and other evidence from scientific research now reveal:

- What managers expect of their subordinates and the way they treat them largely determine their performance and career progress.

- A unique characteristic of superior managers is their ability to create high performance expectations that their subordinates fulfil.

- Less effective managers fail to develop similar expectations, and, as a consequence, the productivity of their subordinates suffers.

- Subordinates, more often than not, appear to do what they believe they are expected to do.'[4]

Professor Livingston goes on to give a number of examples of business groups and individuals in which the high expectation of the manager resulted in superior performance. In one instance the sustained increase in performance (measured by sales results) was as high as 40 per cent. In another, a man – a former hospital porter – whose IQ was lower than that thought necessary even for typing became the successful manager of the main biomedical computer room at Tulane University.

Self-image – a key personal pattern

In Chapter 3 I introduced the concept of self-image, and emphasized the role that it played in our judgements and reactions; and, throughout this book it has appeared, explicitly or implicitly, in a variety of contexts.

It is convenient to think of self-image as existing on a scale from low to high. But, of course, it is much more complex than that. We have, for instance, self-images about whether we are kind people, or competent at mechanical tasks, or good administrators, and so on. The existence of the self-image does not guarantee the existence of the quality to which it refers. I might, for instance, have a self-image which tells me that I am a good delegator – but my staff may strongly disagree. That could cause a problem because, as long as that self-image exists, I am unlikely to change my ways. But in general, good self-image acts in a positive way because we try to preserve it, or live up to it, by acting in accordance with it.

The converse is just as important. If we have developed poor self-images – perhaps in general, or perhaps with regard to a particular ability – we can be trapped at a low level of performance. It is very difficult to exceed the self-image we have. We are stuck at the level of our belief we have about ourselves, unless some sufficiently strong experience jolts us out of this, and advances the image.

If I could obtain one wish from the good fairy for each child on the day it was born, it would be that the child should grow up with a healthy, confident, self-image, high enough to make it stretch up to it, and realistic enough to make that possible.

Methods of building self-image in staff

Building a high self-image in staff and enjoying the results of their consequent superior performance is not a simple matter of handing out praise, or stating one's confidence in people's abilities. It is necessary to have, and to communicate, a confidence which is genuine:

> **Miss Murgatroyd was in charge of the invoicing department, and she was concerned about the high error rate on invoices despatched. This made her irritable, and she was always lecturing her staff or ticking them off for mistakes. Discovering that this only seemed to make matters worse, she decided to change tack and to start praising work and expressing confidence in the general abilities of the department. But no one believed her, and performance did not improve. She left matters for a few weeks. Then she selected the better members of her staff and invited them**

to form a special team who would look after the invoices for the more important customers, and those who had particularly complex transactions. She asked her best supervisor to run this team. Within days the standards of work within this group increased dramatically, and were maintained into the future.

Miss Murgatroyd had realized that her original nagging, however justified, was getting her nowhere. We may imagine that the image of low performance which the group had of itself was merely being reinforced. But her attempt to get action through empty praise was rightly seen as a device. It was only when she put her confidence in the better performers into action that progress was made.

The method chosen by Miss Murgatroyd was effective in her particular situation; but there are many ways in which a manager can communicate esteem for a subordinate's work or potential work. Here are a few examples:

Kevin, a sales manager, believes in the rule of 15 per cent. That is, he has realized that his sales people need to be challenged by targets which will stretch them, but will still be within their compass. A target of a 50 per cent increase could well seem unattainable, and therefore useless as a means of motivation. But he genuinely believes that 15 per cent can be achieved, and so he is able to communicate his confidence.

Fifteen per cent is of course only a rule of thumb, but it does indicate a degree of improvement which may be realistic. And it does not only apply to salesmen. Miss Murgatroyd could be looking for a 15 per cent improvement in error rate on invoices. Another manager might give a target of a 15 per cent decrease in the running costs of an operation. A publicity director could be looking for a 15 per cent increase in favourable mentions in the media. But notice that the key to building self-image does not lie in the target setting itself but in the manager's ability to communicate to his staff that they are capable of that higher level of achievement.

Elizabeth is in the habit of sending a brief note to members of her staff who have carried out some task particularly well. She is careful to include the less dramatic achievements which so often get overlooked; and she watches out for instances of a staff member showing an improvement in performance. Her notes are always handwritten, and she takes care to vary her style because she knows that the recipient is likely to show it to colleagues. She never praises in general terms; she is specific about what she admires about the achievement.

While Elizabeth is quite deliberate in her choice of note writing as a method of building image she is aware that her staff could become cynical about this if they think it 'comes with the rations'. Although she reviews to whom she should send notes, on a regular monthly basis, she never does so unless she feels they are really deserved. Personalizing the note confirms to the recipient that she has taken some thought and trouble over it; specifying the nature of the achievement gives the acknowledgement substance (unlike Miss Murgatroyd's first tactic of empty praise), and enables her to reinforce the particular achievement or improvement she regards as important.

John Dareen has responsibility for negotiating substantial purchases of supplies from sub-contractors. In many instances the initial negotiations are carried out by relatively junior members of his staff. But for safety's sake they are given little room for manoeuvre on price; and company regulations require him to countersign any negotiation before the company is bound by its terms. He arranges a presentation for his staff to show them the relationship between what the company has to pay for its supplies and the eventual profit. He then tells them that they are free to negotiate whatever price they feel is, in the circumstances, in the best interests of the company. He cannot change the company regulations but he undertakes to endorse, without further question, any contract they send to him.

That sort of decision takes nerve – after all John's own job is on the line. But provided his staff are intelligent and responsible (and should he be employing them if they're not?) he has every reason to be confident that they will negotiate better prices than they did under the old system. After all, they have been entrusted with full responsibility by someone who clearly believes they will use it well. Notice here that John took the trouble to make sure that his people fully understood the consequences of their responsibility; he would probably not extend the same freedom to a new member of staff until he or she had demonstrated their competence and reliability over a period of time.

Unconscious communication of image

The manager who sincerely believes that members of his staff are capable of superior performance has jumped the first, big hurdle. (The difficulties in developing such a belief in the face of contrary evidence are discussed below.) Demonstrating his expectation through methods similar to those described will take some thought and ingenuity – related to the situation and personalities involved – but this is quite easy. Just as importantly, he will be, perhaps unconsciously, showing his confidence in a thousand different ways; this requires sincerity. The truth will show in his physical attitudes to his staff, even in the way he greets them in the morning; in his willingness to delegate responsible tasks; in the constructiveness of his criticism of their work. And he will do so in accordance with his own personality:

Munro was a rather formidable Scotsman. He demanded a great deal from his staff, and was very sparing in his praise. One morning he was inspecting the work of an operative who had often been in trouble for his mistakes in the past. He was silent, as usual, but at the end of his inspection he said tersely: 'That's not bad. One of these days you'll make a tolerable engineer.' Then he moved on. To have the makings of a tolerable engineer, in Munro's eyes, was a

mark of extreme praise, and the operative valued it all the more because it was so rare and Munro's standards so high.

However Munro has been running a risk. Occasionally managers who do have high confidence in their staff fail to communicate this. Professor Livingston cites an instance of a solid, phlegmatic manager who failed to raise performance despite his confidence in his people's ability. On investigation it was discovered that his staff had no idea of his high opinion of them. This suggests that managers should review the ways in which they communicate their belief in their staff's capacity; they should not take it for granted that their views will be transferred by some sort of telepathy.

Bad images

The other side of this coin is that bad image can be as readily communicated as good. For instance we might assume that the members of Miss Murgatroyd's department who were not in her special group would receive confirmation of their unsatisfactory performance by failing to qualify. If Elizabeth, having once established the practice, fails to send a note acknowledging achievement it may be taken as a sign of her disapproval. A John Dareen who becomes very critical of his negotiating staff and seeks to control their freedom of action even more closely will certainly convey the idea that he does not find his people trustworthy. And bad image can come about quite simply from neglect:

> **Seamus recruited Charles Graze as an administrative assistant. After a few weeks of work together he realized he had made a mistake in his choice; Graze did not have the qualities for the job. Instead of squaring up to the situation Seamus began, almost unconsciously, to use Graze less and less, and rarely to consult him. Graze got the message quite quickly, and soon began looking for another job. That was, of course, what Seamus really wanted; but was it a good way to deal with the problem?**

Building on qualities rather than defects

This leaves one big difficulty. If it is necessary to have a high opinion of a person in order to communicate a better self-image which will result in superior performance, what happens if you actually have a low opinion?

The answer, on paper and occasionally in practice, is that nothing can be done – and the individual must be invited to leave or to transfer to less demanding work. But, strange as it may seem, this often has more to do with the manager than with the subordinate. Some managers find it difficult to see good qualities; others find it quite easy. And the second type of manager will work on those good qualities, however few they may be, and use them as a way of developing performance.

A useful exercise is to take a number of members of your staff and to list all their good points. However great the temptation, you must omit any bad points, or any qualification of the good points. This can be a difficult exercise to do, but it is very rewarding. Despite yourself, perhaps, you will find your opinion of the people you choose rising, and you will also have a positive base on which you can build their self-images. Only the most courageous should attempt the second part of the exercise: applying it to yourself.

We might imagine that Miss Murgatroyd has a clerk who is accurate in her work, but rather slow. One day an urgent invoice arrives by hand. She takes the opportunity of asking the clerk if she can process this in 20 minutes (which might just be 15 per cent quicker than it would normally take her). If the clerk rises to the challenge Miss Murgatroyd has the opportunity to praise her for being able to work fast as well as accurately. One such instance would probably have only a marginal effect, but if she reinforces the message whenever similar chances arise she can expect the clerk's speeds to rise substantially.

Miss Murgatroyd's approach accords with the findings of a study of appraisal interviews carried out at General

Electric.[5] This established that negative criticism ('Your work's accurate, Joan, but it's just not fast enough') tended to worsen performance in the area criticized rather than to improve it; and the lower the self-image of the interviewee the more marked the effect. On the other hand, the setting of mutually agreed goals for performance ('Do you think you could get this one done in 20 minutes, Joan?') could be very beneficial.

Do *you* need a new team?

You may have noticed that some managers always seem to have excellent teams working for them. Sometimes it's just luck but, if you watch them through their careers, it seems to happen again and again. Could it be that they are using the secret of supercharging staff performance, and getting extraordinary results from quite ordinary people? So, if you think your team is not up to scratch, changing them may not be the answer. Try changing how you look at them instead.

Summary

- A most important factor in people's performance is the self-image they are living up, or down, to. Superior self-image creates superior performance.

- A manager has the influence to help his staff build or modify their self-images. He can do this *constructively* by communicating positive images in line with the task; or *destructively* by communicating bad self-images through negative criticism or attitudes.

- Communicating a good opinion of people's work cannot be done insincerely. A manager must look out for the good points (even if these are few), and then build on them. Usually his real beliefs about his people will be expressed naturally and subconsciously – although inexpressive managers should be aware that they may have to make particular efforts to do this.

- In addition a manager should review his regular practices to ensure that he has ways in which his good opinions are regularly communicated. The ways he will choose will depend on the work situation and his own personality.

9 Delegation Without Tears

Managers use delegation constantly in carrying out their responsibilities. But much delegation in business is badly handled, resulting in frustrated delegates and dissatisfied managers. This chapter looks at the difficulties of delegation, and describes the methods which must be used if it is to be effective. Effective delegation is a skill which increases the manager's span of control and his influence within the business.

Delegation is the way in which a manager multiplies his effectiveness. Without delegation his output can never exceed what he can achieve in a working day; with delegation his output will be multiplied by the number of his delegates. The principle is simple, and at the heart of management. Yet you and I know that delegation is usually done badly. Have you had any of these experiences?

- Your boss asks you to undertake a job. He is rather vague about the details and you gather it will be left very much up to you. When you have completed the job your boss tells you that, after all, he wanted it done differently. It looks to you as if he only discovered how he wanted the job done when he had seen how you tackled it.

- This time, to your initial relief, your boss seems to know what he wants you to do. But, by the time he has gone through all the details, you feel that you are really being used like a machine to carry out his wishes;

there is no opportunity for you to use your initiative in any way.

- Your boss seems to have briefed you quite well for the job, and you're confident you can do it. But, rather annoyingly, he keeps very close to you throughout, asking questions and making suggestions. You begin to suspect that he regrets having delegated the job to you, and would rather be doing it himself. You just wish that he would either take the job back or go away and leave you to it.

- As you progress with the job you have been given, you realize that you are not sure about the limits of your authority. You do not know which decisions you can take on your own, nor which decisions should be referred to your boss. You have an uneasy feeling that you're being asked to guess about this, and that if you make a mistake you will be criticized for not seeking clearance.

- You have completed the job – and you think you've done quite well, but, since no clear criteria for success were ever given, you're not sure. Your boss thanks you, but he gives you no idea of how he thinks you've done. So you don't have any way of improving your performance for the future.

- You were delegated a task and performed it well. You know your boss is pleased. But, to your chagrin, you realize that, outside your area of work, your boss is taking the credit. You appear to have enhanced his reputation and done little for your own.

We have all suffered from bad delegation. But the question is: how good are *we* at delegation? Do any of our subordinates suffer bad delegation from us? Unfortunately most of us are not very good at recognizing when we inflict on others the very things which we resent when they are inflicted on us. Several studies have shown that, at each level of the hierarchy, bosses overestimate their understanding of their subordinates' needs and problems, while resenting the lack of understanding from their own bosses. Most of us do not have what Robert Burns described as the gift of seeing ourselves as others see us. Our feelings operate as a selective filter, enabling us to avoid what our reason would tell us if we let it.[1]

The emotions of delegation

I have written in earlier chapters of the human fear of loss of control, which is rooted in our stored patterns. But control can be lost in two ways: when someone removes it from us, and when we voluntarily cede it through delegation. The difficulty is well known on the historic scale: what happens if you give the vote to women?; what happens if you give that colony independence? And we know it on the family scale: what happens if you allow your teenager to decide what time to come home? Yet delegation means loss of control – otherwise there's no point in it.

In Chapter 3 I quoted J. Pierpont Morgan's remark: 'A man generally has two reasons for doing a thing; one that sounds good and a *real* one.' But in our reluctance to yield control the reason which sounds good will often have substance: liberated colonies often do go through long and troubled periods; teenagers do abuse their freedoms and come to harm. And when we delegate we know we run the risk of the outcome not matching up to our required standards. It is often hard to know how much of our reluctance to delegate is based on sound reasons and how much is based on our instinctive, and perhaps inappropriate, feelings.

A second pattern which can play a part is the loyalty we have to our own ideas. It may not be easy to watch a subordinate take on a task and perform it quite differently from the way we think it should be done, or perhaps from the way we actually did the same task before we decided to delegate it. There is a strong temptation to equate 'differently' with 'worse', and it may be a hard exercise in humility to accept that one's subordinate's performance is just as good, and sometimes better, than one's own.

Unfortunately we cannot switch off such non-rational patterns even when we realize they are interfering with good management; the best we can hope to do is to recognize them for what they are, and to make allowances for them. However, sufficient practice with good delegation can modify such feelings and bring them more into line with reality.

Contributing factors

A factor which may contribute to fears is previous experience of delegation. Most managers have had at least one instance in which delegating a task ended disastrously. This may have been the result of chance, or it may have arisen because, unknowingly, it was handled in the wrong way. But it was enough to reinforce the stored pattern of reluctance – and confirmed the homespun dictum that if you want a job done properly you had better do it yourself.

A second factor can arise from what we feel others expect of our performance. If, for instance, you have a boss who demands that your work should follow his requirements very precisely, you will have good reasons not to take the risks involved in delegation. It may not be your immediate boss's fault, of course, because his own boss may be treading on *his* heels. Good delegation in an organization is a chain reaction usually starting at the top; it takes courage to break the chain at a lower level.

Arguably there are only three positions in any organization – the very top, the very bottom, and all those in between. Those in between share the common circumstance of having to answer to someone above them and of being responsible for the work of someone below them. And whether you are very near the top of a large organization or very near the bottom the most important single factor in your work happiness will be the nature of your boss. It is also a myth that greater responsibility brings greater tensions. On virtually every measurement of management stress, middle managers suffer to a greater extent than senior managers. It is easy to see why. Middle managers have less control

over their own destinies, are less clear about their authority, are subject to more conflicting forces, have less information than senior managers. Each of these limitations conflicts with basic human needs stored in the patterns of the brain. But the myth of senior management stress continues simply because senior managers have the power to preserve it, and every reason to do so.[2]

The responsibility of delegation appears at its most dramatic when a senior person in politics or business finds himself bound to resign because of mistakes at lower levels in the organization which he could not, in the normal way, have known about. It is disconcerting to accept that you must yield control to others, yet retain responsibility for the outcome. No wonder we are often reluctant to do so, or – more commonly – reluctant to do so completely. And half-delegation is the worst of all worlds: we try to retain control while pretending to delegate; thus we substantially reduce the chances of our subordinate being successful while, at the same time, losing the benefits which might have come from doing the job ourselves.

Solving the dilemma of delegation

There is no complete solution because the dilemma is real: we either accept the risks of loss of control or we lose the benefits of multiplying our effectiveness through delegation. Having recognized this, it is only sensible to make sure that we minimize the risks by scrupulously observing the principles of good delegation.

Defining the job and the person

If I had space to give only one principle of good delegation it would be to think through the job first. With a simple, one-off, task this might only take a few minutes; with a long and complex task it might take several days – including re-thinking and revising your initial ideas until you're sure you have it right. This preparation time is essential because your delegate will never have a clearer idea of what you expect of him than you have yourself. Time and hard thought invested now will pay off many times over in the future.

Unless the task is very simple, discipline yourself by writing down the main points. It will help you to focus, and will be an *aide mémoire* for briefing your delegate. I will give the main stages in note form at this point, filling them out when I describe the actual briefing stage which follows selection of the delegate.

- Set out the objectives which you want your delegate to achieve; they may be broad or detailed according to the job – but they must be clear. Specify the standard of performance of objectives so that both of you will know when they have been satisfactorily achieved.

- List the resources which will be needed to fulfil the task, for instance, the level of authority needed, the manpower, the equipment, the office space, the budget.

- List the limits of authority which you think are needed. This would cover: ground rules which are to be observed, specifying what matters should be referred to you before finalization, clearances required from other authorities, e.g. lawyers. Remember that, without limits of authority, your delegate is entitled to achieve his objectives entirely in his own way; this may not be what you want.

- Outline a timetable for achievement of objectives.

- Consider how you are going to supervise the delegation. You might want regular report meetings, or only reports when particular objectives have been reached. What kind of reports are you going to require?

Selecting the delegate

Job selection is notoriously difficult, and this is not the place for a full description of its principles. But the following points may assist you to keep a clear head:

- Using your preparation notes, list the characteristics and skills you believe the job requires. Distinguish between those which are essential and those which are desirable.

- Remember that essential characteristics mean just that. If a candidate lacks any one of them, he is automatically excluded.

- Avoid the temptation of defining a candidate who is a copy of yourself.

- If, as is often the case, you have a specific candidate in mind take care that you do not bend your list of essential characteristics to enable him to qualify.

- On the other hand, few candidates will be ideal. (And none will match up to your abilities!) Look for potential – people have a rewarding habit of growing into jobs.

Briefing

With a clear idea of the job, and a candidate in whom you have confidence, you are in a position to undertake the crucial stage of briefing. Prepare carefully for this, and check that you are ready to deal with all the stages noted in your preparation document:

- Objectives
- Standards
- Resources
- Limits of authority
- Supervision

Objectives and standards

Your preparatory work will enable you to communicate the task to be done. Because you are clear about this in your own mind, you will convey a clear picture to the delegate of what precisely is required of him. This will have been achieved when you and the delegate have agreed objectives and standards which will enable both of you to know whether the task has been successfully completed. The mnemonic CROW will remind you of the essential steps in setting objectives for delegation:

- **C stands for concrete.** Compare an objective like: 'I want you to produce a good in-house magazine' with 'I want you to produce a quarterly in-house magazine which will interest all our staff, and will cover both our business successes and the social side of the company.' The first expression of the objective is too vague; it conveys no more than a general idea of what you have in mind. The second expression, while needing more detail than I have given here, is concrete. The listener has a much clearer idea of what is expected. Concrete objectives are usually longer than vague ones simply because they are more specific and precise.

  In many instances the concrete expression of an objective proves very difficult, but most of the difficulties arise because we are not clear in our own minds exactly what we intend. And the vaguer the objective, the more likely it is that our delegate will not know what is required of him, and that we will be dissatisfied with the result.

- **R stands for realistic.** Remember the motivation calculus in Chapter 3. Unless the individual can see how the actions he will take will lead to the required result, he cannot be motivated. Asking him to ensure that the new magazine is the best in the industry may not be realistic, but asking him to ensure that it matches up to the quality of some respected competitors may well be.

- **O stands for observable.** If an objective is concrete its accomplishment is usually observable. Always check for this because unless the delegate knows what counts as a successful outcome he will lack the satisfaction and motivation which come from measurable achievement. Continuing with our example, you might propose that a readership survey be conducted after the first four issues to test the interest of staff in the magazine. Observable standards have an additional importance if the job requires the delegate to complete preliminary objectives as a first stage before going on further. He must have a measurable way of knowing where he is so that he can move forward to the next stage.

- **W stands for worthwhile.** Occasionally an executive is tempted to delegate a task simply because it has become unimportant to him, or has become tedious. It is right, of course, to offload tasks which can be carried out at a lower or a cheaper level, but a delegate will only respond well if he senses that his boss sees the job as important – that he is being entrusted with a part of the business that really matters. Neither threats nor rewards will ensure that the work is carried out well; he needs the motivation which comes from understanding that his contribution has real meaning.

A fuller discussion of CROW appears in my *Managing People and Problems* (Gower, 1988).

Your preliminary brief should guide you away from setting objectives and standards which are unnecessarily detailed. In some work situations close precision may be necessary, but in others a broader brief will be permissible, and therefore desirable. Your aim should be to describe the outcomes which are expected (remembering that you both need to be concrete about these and how they are to be judged), leaving your delegate the freest hand possible in deciding how to achieve them. This may properly include the possibility of modifying objectives as a result of experience, or because an aspect of the situation changes. People are sometimes reluctant to subscribe to definite objectives because they know that in human affairs they will need room to manoeuvre; but if they see the objectives as re-negotiable whenever necessary – as a planned change rather than unnoticed slippage – then they will be more prepared to make the initial commitment.

Having the maximum latitude to decide how the job should be done is important if the delegate is to 'own' his job.

Human beings are not very good at being machines and if you want to program your delegate completely you would be better served using a computer. But if you want his commitment, his creativity and his intelligence he must have plenty of space in which to exercise these. Your briefing will have identified the limits within which he can make decisions, and these should be clear. But within these limits, and in line with the objectives, he must own the job and take responsibility for it.

Avoid, as far as possible, communicating objectives on tablets of stone. The delegate should be encouraged to discuss and question the objectives you propose, and contribute to their final formulation. You will recall from Chapter 3 how ownership grows through discussion and modification of ideas; and, as ownership grows, so does the sense of being in control rather than of being controlled. Ideally the delegate should leave the briefing with a sense that his objectives are shared between him and his boss, and developed by both of them as a team.

Take special care with the delegate who is reticent. Too often a delegate will leave a briefing professing himself to be clear about his objectives, only to reveal later that he found them incomplete or confusing. A thorough discussion and agreement of objectives will help, but the delegate must also be positively encouraged to ask questions or raise perceived difficulties. A useful method is to test his understanding by asking him how he sees aspects working out. For instance: 'Joe, we've agreed that you'll achieve a balance between business coverage in the magazine and the social side, but what kind of proportions do you think would be right?' He must understand that, just as you have a responsibility to explain the job, he has the responsibility of making sure he has understood the explanation. This can be reinforced if you ask him to come back in a day or two so that he can discuss the objectives again, after he has had time to think them through and see how they would apply.

Timetable

By now your delegate should know what he has to achieve

and the standards required. He must also know by when. Sometimes the date for completion is fixed by outside circumstances, and the only point for discussion will be the timetable of stages to lead towards this. Sometimes there will be room for overall flexibility; but, even in these cases, a timetable is necessary as part of a businesslike framework. But timetables, like objectives, should not be straitjackets. The first timetable is usually no more than an estimate, providing a useful monitor rather than a stick for beating.

Resources

You will have considered these in your initial brief. It is foolish to ask someone to undertake a task and not give him the resources by way of authority, manpower, money, etc. which are needed for him to complete it. Yet this often happens, and the delegator finds himself being badgered for additional resources by a delegate who is spending time with his begging bowl rather than doing the job. Discuss the resources with your delegate until both of you are happy that the job can be done. If circumstances change and more resources are needed, either provide them without lengthy argument or change the objectives to suit the resources. If the shortfall results from an underestimate of what would be required, who bears the blame – the boss who decided the nature of the job or the delegate who was given the job?

Notice that training for the delegate is also a resource. I discuss this further below.

Limits of authority

Julius Caesar is reputed to have said that he would rather be headman in a village than second in command in Rome. This is a good principle: delegate a *complete* job, however small, rather than a half job, however large. It often appears easier, for instance, to give authority for an objective to more than one person. But the result is that no one undertakes full ownership and no one can be held responsible. If two people are needed, one must be responsible – or the job must be split into two parts, each complete in itself. Another way of delegating a half job is to require so many clearances and approvals that the job is sure to be done twice, once by the delegate and once by the delegator. In practice, the job will not even be done once: the delegate will begin to take less trouble since he thinks that the real checking and decision making will be done by someone else; the delegator will not be thorough because he feels entitled to leave the detail to the delegate – and besides his decision to delegate was made because he did not have time to do the job in the first place.

Just as the village headman has his authority limited to the village so the delegate will have a limited authority. The delegator will have considered at his preparation stage what can properly be within the delegate's authority and what must be referred back to him. He should be inclined to give as broad an authority as possible, making sure that the limits are set by rational judgement rather than by his reluctance to cede control; and it may be quite proper to extend these limits as the delegate gains experience and gives the delegator confidence. The cardinal mistake is to be vague about this, leaving the delegate unsure as to what has to be referred and what he can decide for himself. Most often the source of this mistake lies in the, perhaps unconscious, wish of the delegator to cover his rear. If something goes wrong he can always blame the delegate for failing to get his approval; and if it all goes well he can take the credit. Thus he can decide whether he was in the driving seat with the benefit of hindsight.

Supervision

The degree of frequency and the closeness of supervision will vary with the circumstances, but it is important to settle at the beginning how this will be done. Usually it will be defined by the objectives and the timetable. If the delegator, as I have suggested, is only concerned with the completion of objectives and not with the exact means used for achieving them he has no reason to meddle at earlier stages. Indeed, there may be a danger in doing this: he will be tempted to insert his own ideas (usually expressed as a suggestion, but taken as a command), and responsibility will, unnoticed, begin to leak out of the delegate and drip back into the delegator. What was formerly a full job is soon reduced to a half job – with its attendant consequences.

One probable consequence of, even well intended, interfering with a delegate's work is that he will actually become less capable. This psychological effect, described briefly in Chapter 2, is known as learned helplessness. Having a superior looking over one's shoulder and continually demonstrating how the job might have been done just that little bit better, can destroy self-esteem, and reduce the most able person to incompetence.

But rationing supervision is no reason for abandonment. The delegator should be taking an interest in what is happening, and always be ready to discuss difficulties or ideas. But he must keep a tight rein on himself. Delegates will be inclined (at least in the short term) to offload the decisions they have been asked to take. The delegator can make suggestions of course, provided they are not interpreted as decisions, but he should prefer to help the delegate to find good solutions by getting him to explore possibilities rather than by suggesting them.

Supervision should be seen as a positive contribution to the work, not as a negative check. If objectives have been well defined both people will know if they have been achieved, but the delegate will still require an acknowledgement of this; it is an important part of his reward and therefore of his motivation. If the objective has been missed then the reasons for this can be discussed and matters put right. No doubt there will be occasions when the delegate has fallen down on the job through his own fault, and this may call for disciplinary action. But this will be very rare; more often the difficulty lies in some aspect of the selection or briefing which now needs to be corrected through mutual discussion.

Training

The principles of delegation have emphasized that, within the limits set out in the briefing, the delegate takes full responsibility for the task, being answerable only for the fulfilment of agreed, concrete objectives in accordance with a timetable. But it is quite consistent with these principles for the delegate to undergo a period of training before he takes up his responsibilities. This training can be given in a variety of ways from formal training courses to guided and supervised work. Until the training is over responsibility has not been delegated, and the point when this occurs should be clearly marked so that the transfer of responsibility is definite and complete.

My former branch manager, Frank Smith, was often asked by the company to train new managers. His method was to list all the duties of a manager and then allocate half of these to the trainee for six months. During this time he would give instruction and supervision which he gradually relaxed as experience was gained. For the second six months the other half was allocated. When the year was up the trainee took over a different branch, with sole control and authority.

Through such training the delegator can bridge the gap through which the delegate may fall if he does not already have the skills and experience he needs for the task. By providing a model of what is required he gives the delegate a standard which, though not binding him once he has taken over his responsibility, will give him a base point from which he can improve.

Credit where it's due

It seems ironic that, while you will rightly be blamed by your superiors if your delegate does badly, you must be generous with credit when he does well. You are of course entitled to the credit for good delegation, but credit for the task itself, including notation in personnel files if appropriate, must go to the person who has done it. If you do not give proper credit what likelihood is there that your delegate will undertake another task with similar enthusiasm? And if you get a reputation for taking the credit yourself how readily will others undertake delegation from you?

Coming full circle

You may like to glance back at the beginning of this chapter where I listed some of the bad experiences most of us have had when we were delegated tasks. Would you have had those bad experiences if the principles of good delegation had been followed? How will your delegates benefit from your observation of the principles?

Summary

- Delegation multiplies the effectiveness of the manager and is therefore an important tool. Yet the experience of receiving delegation shows that it is often done badly. Many managers fail to learn from this experience when they delegate to others.

- The stored patterns concerning loss of control and the preference people have for their own ideas make delegation emotionally difficult. It is hard to distinguish this from rational caution about delegation. Previous bad experiences and pressures from superiors can contribute to this reluctance. The solution of half-delegation where effective control is retained by the delegator achieves the worst of both worlds.

- The essence of delegation is the transfer of control for a task or a function to another person. This can only be achieved if both delegator and delegate are agreed about what is required, and if the delegate has the qualities and resources to achieve the objectives.

- The first step in good delegation is to think through the job carefully, paying attention to all the factors which will be covered in briefing the delegate. Selection of the delegate must be as objective as possible, measuring him against the demands of the job. The ideal delegate can rarely be found, but there can be no compromise over qualities judged to be needed.

- Briefing the delegate will cover objectives, standards, resources, limits of authority, timetable, supervision.

Objectives and standards: objectives should conform to CROW – concrete, realistic, observable, worthwhile. A good test is to ask: how would we both know that this objective had been accomplished? Care should be taken to define objectives in a way which leaves the delegate maximum freedom of decision, and they should be discussed fully to ensure that the delegate accepts and understands them.

Resources: adequate resources of various kinds must be made available, and there should be agreement about this.

Limits of authority: these should be defined clearly at this stage, although they may be extended with experience. It is better to delegate a limited job completely than to half-delegate a bigger job.

Timetable: this should be set and agreed.

Supervision: the timing and nature of reports should be defined. While the delegator should take a continual interest in the work he must avoid the danger of controlling it over the delegate's shoulder. Supervision should be used as a positive aid to achievement not as a negative monitor.

- For some jobs the delegator will require training, and various methods may be appropriate. During this period delegation has not taken place, and the eventual transfer of authority must be definite.

- The delegator is entitled to the credit for good delegation, but the delegate gets the credit for the job he has undertaken. Without this, motivation is removed and delegation will become difficult.

10 Presentations and Reports

The ability to make competent, spoken presentations to large and small groups is essential to an executive who wants to get his own way in business, and present himself as a leader. While natural talent helps, virtually everyone can learn to be an effective speaker through using the basic rules of good presentations. These are based on understanding the differences between spoken and written communication, and on understanding the patterns through which audiences absorb the speaker's message. This chapter deals with the key points of constructing a presentation – from the initial research to the final touches which transform the worthy but dull into the interesting and persuasive. The most important skills of delivery are described. A section on applying the principles of good presentation to written reports concludes the chapter.

For a moment there is silence. In front of you is an audience looking at you with polite interest; at your hand is a sheaf of notes and some overhead projector transparencies; in your head there is – or, until a few moments ago, there was – the brainchild you are about to present. Your performance over the next half-hour will decide whether your idea is stillborn or whether it will be implemented, to your credit and to the advantage of your firm.

You are about to make a presentation.

If you feel nervous it's scarcely surprising. Studies have shown that people rate speaking in public as a more frightening experience than height, loneliness, sickness and even death.[1] Moreover you will be aware that, in a business situation, a good performance can enhance your personal standing, your authority, and your fitness for higher office, while a bad performance can damage all these – perhaps irretrievably. The impression created, bad or good, will have a strong impact and strong impacts remain in the minds of the listeners, affecting their judgement for a long time to come.

You may have wondered why some speakers respond well to audiences; they are stimulated by them, they exude great confidence, their minds work well and they become more articulate – while others become tongue-tied, their brains freeze and their normal coherence dissolves. Just like the cockroach (see Chapter 1 and chapter note 2) the presence of an audience arouses the whole nervous system. If the speaker is basically confident of his performance this will stimulate him and sharpen his ability, but if he lacks confidence his heightened nervous arousal will inhibit his performance and paralyze his faculties.[2]

There is, therefore, every reason for the manager who wants to get his own way in business to become a competent public speaker. To do this he does not have to discover a great new talent inside himself, but only to pay attention to the key principles for making good presentations, and to prepare himself according to them. Certainly some people have a natural flair for public speaking, and they are fortunate. But, in preparing speakers over many years, I have never yet encountered anyone who could not make at least a competent presentation by using the principles I will describe in this chapter. In my experience the ratio of poor presentations to good is about ten to one, so a competent presenter is an invaluable asset to a business, and a person to watch.

Chapter structure

The first part of this chapter is divided into five sections, each of which is preceded by a brief overview:

1 WHY SPOKEN PRESENTATIONS ARE
    DIFFERENT
2 PRELIMINARY STEPS

3 A GOOD STRUCTURE
4 DECORATING THE PRESENTATION
5 SPEAKING SKILLS

1 WHY SPOKEN PRESENTATIONS ARE DIFFERENT

There are several reasons for giving presentations, such as conveying information to a large number of people simultaneously or getting approval for an idea from a management committee. But the speaker must realize that the characteristics of presenting to a group differ in many respects from presenting to an individual. Audiences require very special treatment if they are to be influenced. However the nature of their responses allows the speaker to make great use of their stored patterns, and so to convey powerful messages.

In business, presentations are made to groups, large and small, for very practical reasons. If you want to convey a message to 500 people all at the same time, you hire a hall and you tell them. It is true that you can put the information on paper and distribute 500 copies. But it is unlikely that you will have 500 eager readers. Currently (1990) you would expect to pay between £300 and £400 to attend a two-day study conference given by a specialist organization. Yet such a conference would contain less than a tenth of the information available in a book like this. On a rough calculation information obtained through conference presentations costs 200 times as much as reading it in a book. That is the measure of business people's reluctance to undertake the effort of reading and private study. It is certainly not for the quality of the lunch – which is either poor, or good enough to ensure that you doze off in the afternoon.

Presentations to smaller groups owe less to the reluctance of people to read. Usually the intention is that the group will work immediately with the material presented. This might be a management group which must take a decision, or perhaps a work team requiring a briefing. Here the chief value is that the group gets all the information at the same time, it has an opportunity to question the presenter, and can then discuss its reactions as a group, perhaps arriving at a decision as a result.

It would be wrong, however, for the students of good presentation to assume that, in practice, spoken presentations are equivalent to written material. They contain some marked characteristics, both positive and negative, which make them very different.

Positive and negative characteristics

- A presentation focuses communication on a given moment in time. Your 500-strong field force are combined as a group in front of you. They will react as a group and will be emotionally influenced by this; a fine presentation can change the future course of the company in a way which material read by the same number individually could never do. A presentation to a smaller group, say, a board of directors, will have a different objective. You will be using the occasion of the presentation to bring matters to a head. The presentation becomes a focused opportunity for action and decision.

- The presenter has great control over the information he transmits, the pace of transmission, and the order in which he transmits it. The reader of written material can choose his own pace, he has time to criticize the content, and he can change the order by reading over passages at will.

- The presenter is able to address the stored patterns of his audience very directly. His individual listeners will simply not have the time to reflect on whether they wish to apply a more analytic judgement to what they hear, and they will be inhibited from this by the collective response of the group. (The larger the group the more exactly it will conform to standard patterns.)

- The presenter controls the emotional impact of his points through the techniques he employs. With experience he can sense the feedback of the audience and adjust to their visceral responses. The direct contact between his personality and that of the audience can be a powerful additional factor in persuasion.

- Audiences have a tendency to be passive receivers; that is, they are disinclined to use their minds. Consequently the presenter has to work very hard at simplifying his material, and making it intelligible enough for the audience to grasp his meaning.

- Audiences retain very little of what they hear. Ask a member of an audience for a summary of the presentation 24 hours later and you will find that only a miscellaneous point or two is recalled. Consequently a presenter must take considerable pains to make sure his material is not only heard but assimilated.

- Conversely, the presenter can make sure that his audience does not recall information which he needs to give but would prefer that they did not retain.

- Audiences need to be strongly motivated to listen at all; and they need continually to be stimulated to retain their attention.

- Good written communication requires good writing, but this may be delegated. A presenter can be helped to prepare his material, but only he can give it; and skills vary.

I have not attempted to distinguish positive characteristics from negative characteristics in this list. It rather depends on your point of view. However each one has something to teach about good presentations, as this chapter will show.

2   PRELIMINARY STEPS

The first stage of preparing a presentation is to define the objective. This will then act as a guide to the whole of the presentation.

You should know, or discover, as much as you can about your

*audience. What are their expectations? What are their atti-
tudes? What are the likely patterns to which you can appeal?*

*Assemble the points you want to make in support of your
objective. Take your time over this, and be ready to prune so
that you can concentrate on giving a few key points the
maximum impact. By this stage a structure for your
presentation will be beginning to emerge.*

Define the objective

The characteristics of the presentation which I have listed
indicate that the presenter needs to be very clear about what
effect he wishes to have on his audience. If I were able to
give a presenter just one piece of advice, worth all the rest,
it would be: *ask yourself what you want to have happened to
your audience between the time you stand up and the time
you sit down.* Notice that the question asks what happens to
the *audience*, not what happens to *you*. The objective relates
to the audience; and it will dictate to you the means which
you will use to achieve it.

Start with a sheet of paper, and write down your objective.
You will probably find that it has several parts, some more
important than others. Remember the CROW criteria (see
Chapter 9 if you have forgotten). Keep your sheet of paper
by you as you prepare your presentation; check continually
that the methods you are considering support that objective
and do not detract from it. Accept that, unless you have a
clear objective in your mind, and use this to guide your
presentation, your success will depend only on luck. And
the odds are not on your side. Here is an example of how
your objective might look:

**You want to persuade the senior management group to
accept your proposals for a new publicity campaign. Your
objective might look like this:**

1. *The group should understand how a higher level of
   publicity would contribute to our sales revenue, and
   eventually pay for itself.*

2. **The group should see the cost of the campaign as proportionate to our other marketing expenses.**

3. **The group should be sufficiently enthusiastic about the proposal to agree that £50000 should be spent for a test campaign, and to authorize the balance of the expenditure if specified results are achieved.**

That is a very businesslike objective (although you will notice that it has an emotional content), but there is no reason why you should not add other items which are personal to you. After all no one else is going to see your piece of paper:

4. **The group should see me as an efficient and competent person, and think of me as someone with a bright future in the company.**

Not all presentations are focused on obtaining a favourable decision; the principle of defining the objectives is the same but the outcome would be different. For instance:

The annual planning process has just been completed and you want to communicate the general company plan to franchise managers in East Anglia so that they can see how their work will contribute to it. Your objective might be:

1. **The managers should be aware of the company's business objectives over the planning period, and understand the main strategies which will lead to their achievement.**

2. **The managers should see how the achievement of their targets will contribute both to their own prosperity as well as that of the company. They should be enthusiastic about this.**

3. **The managers should have increased confidence in the company's capacity and willingness to support them into the future. They should be clear about the support programme being introduced to help them to be more successful.**

4. **The managers should be clear about the next steps required of them in the target-setting process.**

5. *The managers should recognize my personal commitment to them and to the company plan, and my determination to make the plan work well through the help of their contributions.*

Know your audience

In Chapter 4, Persuading the Boss, I stressed the importance of understanding as much as possible about the patterns and the motivations of the person to be persuaded. A presentation to a group requires the same forethought, together with some additional features:

- A one-to-one presentation provides continual, explicit feedback which enables the presenter to modify his approach according to the response. A presentation to a group, because it has been prepared in advance, cannot be modified so easily; therefore anticipating the reaction of the group accurately is relatively more important.

- A group is made up of individuals each of whom has his own stored patterns through which to judge the information received. To this is added the effect of being a member of a group. The group may be large or small, it may be a strongly welded team with shared purposes and values or an uncoordinated group with nothing in common beyond belonging to the same audience. Therefore the presenter must assess the influence of this group factor, and take it into account.

Knowing the small group

The smaller the group the more important its individual members become. Imagine, for instance, presenting a proposition to a senior management committee with only six members. You will need to have made an assessment of the relevant views of each member: what are their motivations, their hidden agendas, their prejudices, their patterns?

But you must go beyond this and consider them in a group context. Who are the decision makers? Who have influence on the others? What is the political interplay – the alliances and tensions – between them? You may know them well as a group – perhaps you have presented to them before. If so, you will have some useful information about their group patterns. If you are meeting them for the first time you may have to apply considerable imagination and judgement to whatever information you have, or can obtain.

Knowing the larger group

Clearly an analysis of the individuals in a group of 500 would be impossible. But you should consider whether there are any categories within the audience who are particularly influential. For instance the branch managers present among an audience of salesmen might be such a category. Understanding group values will be very important for a large audience; you need to know about their experiences, their difficulties, what motivates them, their shared values, their knowledge of the topic you intend to present, and their expectations. If you do not know the group well, research them thoroughly beforehand.

A checklist

As a minimum you should make sure you have obtained the following information before you start your preparation:

- If invited to speak, what are the inviter's objectives? Get these defined along the lines you will use for forming your own objectives.

- What are the audience's likely expectations? Any relevant background? Issues in their minds?

- Expected size of audience.

- General characteristics of audience.

- What are audience doing or hearing before your presentation?

- What are audience doing or hearing after your presentation?
- Length of item, opportunities for questions?
- Will you be chaired? What sort of introduction?
- What kind of room will be used? Is there a dais, lectern?
- What equipment is available – public address system, overhead projector, flipchart, etc? (Never rely on promised felt tip pens, OHP pens, chalks, drawing pins, etc. Bring your own.)
- Will you have an opportunity to survey the room beforehand, and familiarize yourself with the equipment?

Assembling your points

It is hard to know whether to start the preparation of a presentation by considering points first and structure afterwards, or the other way around. In fact the process is circular – the points are both built in to the structure and arise out of it. Personally I try to break into the circle by looking at individual points (believing that the structure will eventually begin to suggest itself); so that is the order I follow here.

Naturally I have my written objectives prominently before me because a point only has value if it relates to these. But beyond this, I like – at the initial stages – to be as random as possible. I allow my mind to float around the objectives and to note likely points (as well as some unlikely ones) as they arise. If I have the opportunity I allow the objectives to lie around in my head over a number of days, attending to them periodically and in a very relaxed way. Sometimes the most valuable points have come into my mind under very informal circumstances – for which there is a respectable precedent in the story of Archimedes who discovered how to measure the volume of irregular objects while sitting in his bathtub.

But eventually I must sit down and get my points into

some sort of order which will fit into a satisfactory structure. I would hope by this stage to have more points than I could possibly use. The operation of pruning them is always painful but the object is to achieve the maximum impact with the fewest points, and in the simplest way. Only the speaker is aware of those stylish points he has had to omit; no one else will miss them. Many more presentations have failed because the speaker has made too many points than because he has made too few.

3   A GOOD STRUCTURE

As a guide for developing structure, bear in mind the nature of audiences. They are passive listeners; and they quickly forget what they have heard unless the speaker helps them to transfer it into long-term memory. Therefore good structure will motivate the audience to attend, will help them to grasp the meaning of what has been said, and will reinforce their memory of the important points.

Audiences will not retain a sequence of points unless they have first been given a simple pattern which connects them together and gives them meaning. Therefore spelling out the intended structure, early in the presentation, is important. In a complex presentation sub-structures may also need to be explained, at the relevant time.

Audience recall is high at the beginning of a presentation, dips in the middle, and rises towards the end. This will affect the order chosen for the presentation, and indicates that particular attention must be paid to maximizing the value of high periods of recall.

The primacy effect can be used to advantage. A speaker has an opportunity to establish a good relationship with his audience at an early point; if he does so, he will get better attention and better acceptance for his ideas. This is the time for the speaker to motivate his audience by convincing them of the importance of what he has to say, and setting up the patterns through which they will view his presentation. The recency effect should also be used. A presentation should be well summarized, and thought should be given to finishing with a powerful and convincing point.

If there are contrary arguments to the speaker's proposition, he must decide whether, and where, he should deal with them. Primacy and recency effects will help him here.

In considering how to present your points, use the sequence – statement, example, inference. It assists meaning and consolidation, while respecting an audience's natural characteristic of not thinking for itself. The emotional overtones of the language used will also have an effect.

Before we look at the question of structure we must examine more closely the effect of a spoken presentation on the audience.

The nature of audiences

Some years ago I gave a presentation to a conference. I flattered myself that I had made a rather good job of it, and it was well received by the audience. Three days later I was telephoned by a delegate. He made some complimentary remarks about my presentation, and then said that he wanted to pass the information on to members of his own organization. He asked me for a copy of the script. I told him that I had no script. He then asked me for a copy of my notes. I told him that my scrappy notes would be incomprehensible to him. He seemed downhearted about this, so I asked him what he had actually remembered about my presentation. It turned out that he could recall practically nothing. So much for the quality of my presentation!

The fact of the matter is that speaking to audiences is a very inefficient way of conveying information unless great care is taken to compensate for the inherent limitations of the medium. If I may remind you of some points I made at the beginning of this chapter:

- Audiences have a tendency to be passive receivers; that

is, they are disinclined to use their minds. Consequently the presenter has to work very hard at simplifying his material, and making it intelligible enough for the audience to grasp his meaning.

• Audiences retain very little of what they hear. Ask a member of an audience for a summary of the presentation 24 hours later and you will find that only a miscellaneous point or two is recalled. Consequently a presenter must take considerable pains to make sure his material is not only heard but assimilated.

• Audiences need to be strongly motivated to listen at all; and they need continually to be stimulated to retain their attention.

In fact these points, which can be summed up as motivation, meaning and memory, are all connected since they arise from the method in which the human mind absorbs information. The method is very efficient for most purposes but it is not well suited to responding to spoken presentations. Fortunately the speaker can take steps to minimize the limitations and even turn them to his advantage. But let's explore the difficulties a little further first.

The short-term memory and the long-term memory

The memory has two layers. If I give you my telephone number, which has nine digits, you will initially hold it in your short-term memory. That will be enough for you to dial the number correctly or repeat it to someone else, provided you do so quickly. But, if you want to remember it permanently you will need to do some more processing. You might repeat it several times; you might write it down, not as a reminder but because the process of writing it down somehow fixes it in the mind; you might try to relate it to some other combination of numbers you know well. All these methods serve to transfer the number into the long-term memory; once there, it can stay for a very long time. The registration number of the car my father owned 50 years ago was FBH 864. But then small boys repeat numbers.

Outside my window as I write is a car I have owned for three years. I have no idea of its registration number.

The short-term memory has a very small capacity; generally it can recall no more than seven to ten unrelated items. Increase the number of items and some of them will be lost – the old items will be replaced by the new ones.

Consider the relevance of this to the spoken word. Information is presented, item after item, for a period of many minutes. Unless the contents of the short-term memory can be quickly transferred into the long-term memory, the information will be lost – replaced by the succeeding information. Contrast this with reading a book which enables you to work at your own pace, to re-read passages, to reflect at the end of sections, to make notes of interesting points. Unless the presenter of spoken information constructs and presents his material in such a way that the listener is able to use his long-term memory, little of what he has said will be recalled.

A first step is *motivating* the audience. Unless its members really *want* to recall the information they are being given they will not bother to transfer it into the long-term memory – just as you will not bother to memorize my telephone number if you expect to have no further use for it. But a presentation may involve a great deal of information, and this means that the attention and alertness of the audience must somehow be retained throughout. The second step is conveying *meaning*. Unless the audience is able to relate the new information to information already existing in their heads, transfer into the long-term memory is almost impossible. The third step is *memory*; the speaker must handle his material in such a way that the audience are helped, and in some instances almost obliged, to make the transfer to long-term memory.[3]

The various aspects of constructing a presentation which I describe below address the needs for motivation, meaning and memory in several different ways.

Structure

'I will begin by describing how Sun Life of Canada has

traditionally worked in the house purchase market. Then I want to talk about some serious threats to our methods of working which have caused us to re-think our strategy. Finally I will describe the solutions we decided to adopt – and how they are working out in practice (micro pause).'

That is an extract from the first section of a presentation I made recently to a group of senior businessmen. I was laying in front of them a structure or a pattern to help them order and understand what I had to say. Instead of a series of points which would no doubt prove to be coherent if they remembered them long enough to reflect on them, I gave them just three things to remember - the previous situation, the new threats, the solution. And those three points had a logical connection between them, making a *pattern* into which they could fit the detailed remarks I would make later. At no stage could they be confused about how what I was saying related to my theme. As I worked through my material I reminded them occasionally of where we were, and as I drew to my close I summarized my remarks within the same framework.

In addition to helping an audience to obtain meaning by giving them a pattern through which to interpret otherwise apparently miscellaneous material, structure is a powerful aid to memory because it enables the audience to classify or group a number of different ideas under a few headings. This operates rather like a good filing system in which a great deal of information can be stored and retrieved by reference to the appropriate heading. But of course we do need to remember the headings and, in my example, I obliged my audience to commit my headings to long-term memory by rehearsing them through appropriate repetition.

My presentation was short. It took about 20 minutes, which is about as long as an experienced speaker can expect to hold the attention of an audience. The late Lord Brabazon of Tara once said that anyone who had so much to say that it took longer than 20 minutes should go away and write a book about it. It also had the advantage of an inherently simple structure or, to be more accurate, I had worked quite hard to adapt a complex issue so that it would have a simple structure. Where the nature of the presentation is obliged to be more complex, spelling out the structure, reminding, and summarizing becomes even more important. Here is an example of how such a presentation might start:

> **'Over the years we have devoted a great deal of energy and money to increasing our market share. But we have not achieved our objective. In this presentation I want to remind you of the main strategies we have used, and to suggest why they have not been fully effective. I will submit to you that they have all suffered from a common flaw. Finally, I want to propose a completely new approach to the problem which avoids this flaw and which promises a real increase in market share.'**

The complexity of this would probably lead you to use sub-structures for individual sections:

> **'I have divided the different strategies we have employed into three main approaches: strategies aimed at raising our profile through advertising; strategies aimed at increasing our branch network; and strategies aimed at making sales through product innovation. Let's take these one by one.'**

The filing system has become a little more extensive but the principle is the same. The detail relates to the sub-structure, the sub-structure relates to the main structure, the main structure is a coherent pattern with meaning. The greater complexity of the material demands even more attention to careful structuring (and other aids, described below, may be necessary) to relieve the memory load imposed on the audience.

Structure and audience recall

Many experiments have been carried out to test the recall of spoken presentations: the items best recalled come from the beginning and the end of the presentation; items from the middle of the presentation are more likely to be forgotten. There is more than one reason for this, but a contributing factor is that the listener has an opportunity to rehearse the earlier items in his mind, transferring them to his long-term memory; similarly, the end section of the presentation, being followed by a break, gives an opportunity for rehearsal.

This means that a presentation which lasts for an hour may cover more ground but will transfer less permanent information than a presentation which takes 45 minutes but is split into sections of fifteen minutes with an allowance for break times. Figure 10.1 shows the effect of this on the recall of an audience – first, for a continuous presentation; second, for a presentation with built-in breaks.[4]

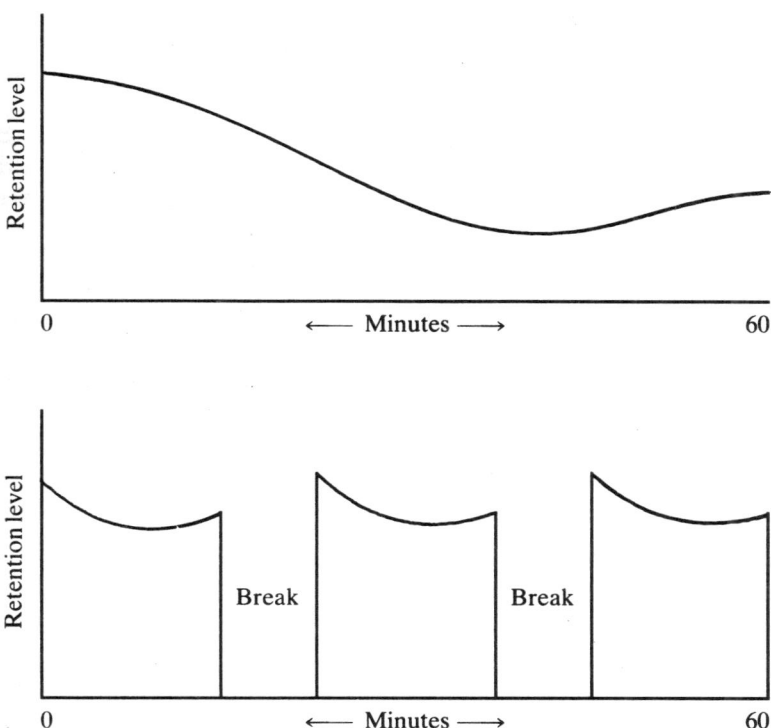

Figure 10.1   Improving audience retention by using breaks

It also follows that micro pauses within the presentation are an aid to rehearsal. The words themselves can be spoken as quickly as is consistent with clarity, but the pauses, albeit of only a second or two after each significant point, enable rehearsal to take place.[5] Particularly significant points will usually be repeated more than once during the course of a presentation, but used, sparingly, immediate repetition can lend great emphasis – perhaps introduced with the words: 'That point is so important, I'll say it again.' This attracts the audience's attention, and forces mental rehearsal on them.

The impact of primacy

You will recall from the early chapters of this book that initial impressions are very powerful; they colour the following sequence of events through encouraging us to look for evidence in support of the first impression and to overlook contrary evidence. Combine this fact with the high recall present at the beginning of a presentation and the need to motivate the audience to listen, and you will realize that the beginning of a presentation is key.

Establishing the speaker's personality

If an audience likes a speaker they warm to him, listen to him, and – more irrationally – they tend to believe him.[6] Many speakers like to open with a little piece of humour since it is easy to like someone who has made you laugh, and the laughter itself binds the group together, reinforcing the ability of the speaker to use the group effect to help him attain his objectives. The formal joke is something of a hazard unless you have a talent for telling such jokes – then your personality will come through. Another method is to make some informal remarks, perhaps related to some circumstance common to the group; it might be something as simple as a reference to the weather or to the difficulty of finding the hotel. A presenter can often make remarks about himself – remarks which help audiences to see him as a person and therefore someone to whom they can relate:

'You will have to forgive me if I look at you a little strangely. I'm wearing bi-focals for the first time. Whenever I tilt my head you all seem to recede – which is rather depressing for a speaker. When I tilt it again you seem to swoop towards me – which is rather threatening. Either way, both you and my notes are out of focus.'

But beware of self-deprecating remarks which endanger your credibility:

'Actually I'm not quite sure why I'm standing up here at all. Most of you in the audience know more about this subject than I do. I can only hope you'll find something of value in what I have to say.'

Such remarks come from a lack of self-confidence – the speaker is trying to protect himself from the threat of his audience. No doubt he will avoid being lynched, but only because, following that remark, most of the audience will fall asleep. After all they've just been told that the presentation is not going to be worth their attention. Other aspects of establishing the right relationship with the audience are a matter of manner rather than the words themselves. I will return to this in due course.

Establishing the audience's motivation

'Ladies and gentlemen, we have reached a critical point in our business affairs. The new legislation can destroy everything we have done, or it can prove to be the biggest opportunity for profitable expansion we have ever had. The outcome will depend on the decisions we take over the next month. My presentation this morning will explain why these decisions are necessary, and outline the different options open to us.'

That opening would, I think, give an audience adequate motivation to listen. But even when the circumstances are less dramatic good motivation must be provided:

'We all want to increase the productivity of our salesmen; it's the quickest way to increase business and profitability. The new training system which I am going to outline for you this morning will enable us to do just that. But subject to just one condition. It will only work if it has the cooperation of every person in this room.'

Here is another approach which depends on curiosity; we are easily motivated to listen to the answer to a question which intrigues us:

'You must often have wondered why our competitors always seem to be a step ahead of us in product innovation. After all, we devote a big budget to research and development, and our people are bright. In fact I suspect there are good reasons for this, and this morning I want to show you why.'

Dr Capra (see Acknowledgements) once started a lecture to his students by showing a slide which announced that, instead of the lecture, an examination which would account for 30 per cent of degree marks was about to be administered. A number of students became belligerent, complaining about unfairness; others became extremely agitated. Dr Capra pointed out that they were exhibiting the classic responses of a threatened group. There was no exam of course, but Dr Capra was able to lecture on the physiological changes in the autonomic nervous system of threatened animals to a very attentive audience – who knew just what it felt like.

It should never be difficult to identify the motivation for people to listen. If you can't identify it, you really have no reason to give a presentation or to ask others to spend time listening to it. The point I am making is that you need to be clear what it is, and to present it in such a way that it brings the audience forward in its seats, wanting to hear more.

The recency effect

Having considered the beginning of a presentation, we should now consider its ending. You will recall that people are inordinately affected by what they have heard most recently, provided the information has enough impact to attract their attention. You will also recall that the attention and memory of an audience rises in the last minutes of a presentation (see Figure 10.1). Good summarizing is necessary to bring the main points to mind so that they are consolidated in the long-term memory. In longer or complex presentations it will be necessary to summarize the various sections, relating them back to the main structure. In such cases the final summary will be the summary of summaries

Look out for the opportunity to make a last, telling point. It will stick in the minds of the audience and have an effect out of proportion to its content. For example:

'I suggested to you when I began speaking that we lagged behind our competitors in product innovation. But there has been one exception. Many of you will recall that about five years ago we introduced an electronic valve which was very successful and has been imitated by our competitors. And you will also remember that the methods we used to develop it were, by coincidence if you like, in line with the principles I have been explaining. What we have done before we can do again.'

Primacy, recency and the contrary argument

Speakers must often decide how to deal with arguments which appear to disprove the case they are making. Rightly they suspect that, if they do not deal with the contrary argument, their listeners will suspend credibility – and indeed be distracted by the presence of the contrary argument in the back of their heads. But, if the contrary argument is stated in the presentation, the audience will be reminded of its force. How should they deal with this dilemma?

The first stage is to decide whether or not the audience is generally favourable to the line of approach you are taking. If so, you may omit contrary arguments (the audience simply don't want to hear anything which conflicts with their existing patterns). If not, then you must deal with the contrary arguments, and show why they are misconceived – or why they do not apply in these particular circumstances. But primacy and recency effects will help you to position them so that they carry the least force with the audience.

The broad rule is to deal with contrary arguments quite early in the presentation. Naturally you will have used the primacy effect to set the main patterns through which you want your audience to interpret your messages. But soon after that you will need to remove any distraction caused by a contrary argument by expounding it (with respect – since many of your audience will hold it), and then dealing with it. You should avoid expressing any contrary arguments towards the end of the presentation, or mentioning them in your summary. You should be using the recency effect to reinforce what you want your audience to remember, not what you would prefer them to forget.[7]

Making your points

Points can be made in several different ways, and will benefit from variety of presentation. But bear in mind a basic sequence which research suggests is particularly effective. There are three stages:

1. Statement
2. Example
3. Inference.

Thus:

> (Statement) 'Our market moves very quickly. If a competitor gets a six month's start with a new feature that the customer likes, they get a lot of new sales at our expense. It's very hard to catch up.
>
> (Example) When Simpsons put in that automatic heat sensor last year their sales figures leapt. We had to reduce our prices to get rid of our stock. By the time we'd introduced our own version a lot of our old customers had switched to Simpsons. And of course Simpsons are still benefiting from the service contracts.

(Inference) If we want to prevent that sort of thing happening again we're going to have to be quicker than Simpsons at spotting new features we can incorporate.'

The rule – *statement, example, inference* – is not arbitrary. The statement by itself may be clear, but giving an example brings it to life and involves the imagination of the listener. He now knows exactly what is meant, and he has begun to incorporate it into his long-term memory. The conclusion continues the process of consolidation but it also presents the audience with the inference they should be drawing. Audiences are very poor at drawing inferences; they have to have this task done for them. It may seem unfair on the speaker to have to do the audience's thinking for them on top of everything else. The consolation is that the speaker can decide what that thinking should be.[8]

Mind your language

'I am a freedom fighter; you are a political agitator; he is a terrorist.'

In Chapter 4 I made the point, with examples, that words carry emotional overtones, and that the English language was particularly rich with variations which can give a different nuance to the message. This covert power of words is particularly effective, for good or ill, in public speaking because the audience has little time to evaluate the bias. Listeners are left with the emotional flavour long after the words or phrases used have been forgotten. Words have power, use them well.

4   DECORATING THE PRESENTATION

Motivation, meaning and memory are all enhanced by decorating the basic presentation to raise the attention and the comprehension of the audience in different ways:

- *using reminder visuals to help attention and recall*

- *speaking in terms of the audience's knowledge so that they can relate new information to what they already know*

- *using well chosen, simple, visuals to help explain or emphasize important or complex points*

- *using variety in manner, material, methods of presentation, audience participation; variety restores lagging attention, raises recall, and enables crucial points to be highlighted – but choose appropriate methods and don't overdo it.*

If it offends anyone to think of business presentations as a branch of show business, it must at least be accepted that show business has a great deal to teach the presenter. Recall some of the techniques that television uses, even in serious documentaries, to retain the audience. There is a great deal of variety: different camera angles and distances, switches of scene, switches of speaker. Visuals are carefully selected to make a point or to provide pleasure. Ideas are simplified so that they can be communicated, and they are often linked to ideas already in the viewer's mind. The key concepts of the programme will be repeated in different ways, and often summed up at the end. Sometimes all this can be irritating to the viewer who happens to be expert in the subject, but the television director knows his audience and he chooses his methods to communicate the maximum which he believes will be possible.

The presenter has different techniques at his disposal – some better and some worse than in television – but the problems are very similar. The television producer has to entertain; it is so easy to switch channels. The presenter's audience can switch channels in the mind, or switch the mind off altogether. For both, entertainment is a means of retaining the attention of the audience so that the objective can be achieved. Similarly, motivation, meaning, and memory are important. Unless the material is designed to satisfy all these, the programme and the presentation will have no impact. The techniques which I describe below should not be regarded as ends in themselves; their use, and the manner of their use, should be judged by the degree to which they will contribute to the objective.

Reminder visuals

To help an audience to know where they are in a complicated presentation reminder visuals can be very helpful. These will normally consist of succinct points which keep the audience on track through their eyes as well as their ears. They can be used at different stages of the presentation, and are particularly useful for summarizing. They should always be very simple; ten points on one visual would be the maximum – two visuals of five points would be better.

Various media can be used, from a blackboard or flip chart to computer programmed slide projection. You may want to use a 'reveal' method, where the points appear on the visual as they are required. In terms of practical effect the blackboard has never been bettered, but nowadays people sometimes feel shortchanged unless they see some technical sophistication. On the other hand too much technical sophistication can defeat its own ends when the audience are left remembering the techniques rather than the content. And they will certainly remember only the techniques if the presenter has not fully tested and mastered them.

In my experience professional producers of visuals for presentations have a voracious appetite for work. Give them a chance and they will illustrate every word of a presentation with an imaginative slide. I once saw this actually done using an advanced method of generating slides by a computer. As a display of technical facility it was admirable, but it was a distraction from the presentation rather than an aid to it.

Visual reminders are a holding device assisting the mental rehearsal needed to get points into the long-term memory. The display will remain up for long enough to allow the eye to rest on the message and transmit it more deeply into the brain. This can be very powerful if the points are actually

written by the presenter (on a flip chart or overhead
projector, for instance) since the brain will follow this
closely, and the period of pause required will give a natural
break for consolidation. But only short and simple points
can be handled in this way. Good, clear handwriting is
essential, and the presenter must practise and time this
beforehand.

An example of a visual giving simple reminder points
appears in Figure 10.2.

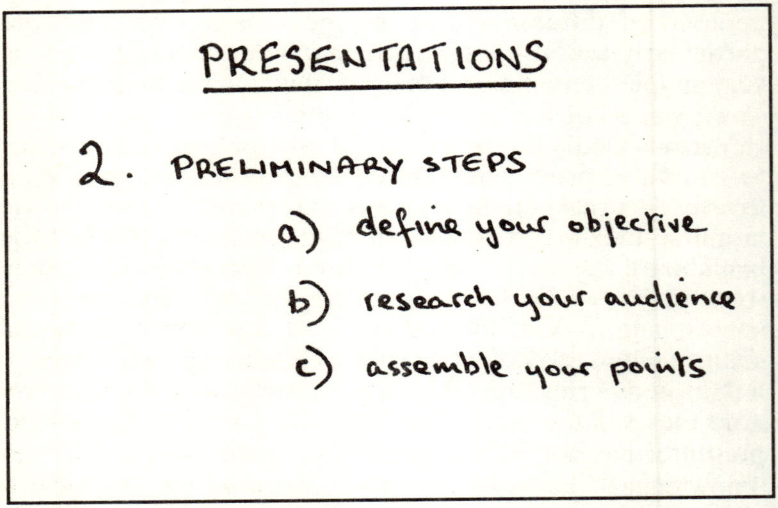

Figure 10.2   Simple reminder visual

Attending to meaning

Structure, as I have described it in the preceding section, is
the way in which the presenter offers to his audience a
framework of meaning, a pattern, which enables them to
understand – as well as to follow – the message he is
delivering. But beyond the pattern imposed by the presenter
there are other patterns in the mind of the audience through
which they will attempt to understand what he is saying. If,
for example, you watch a television documentary on a
subject with which you are familiar, you will find it easy to

understand and easy to recall afterwards. This happens because you are fitting the new information into a pattern or a framework which is already in your mind – you have, so to speak, mental hooks on which to hang it. In Chapter 2 I gave an example of this process when I described how an experienced chess player, in contrast to a non-player, could recall the position of the pieces on the board by relating them to patterns already in his mind.

So your audience will need to use their existing patterns of knowledge to understand what you are saying and to remember it. You must therefore be very aware of what these patterns of knowledge are likely to be. Imagine explaining a new computer operating system to a group of computer experts, and then to a group of laymen. Your approach would need to be completely different. Indeed, even the phrase 'computer operating system' will have conveyed a comprehensible idea to some of my readers, and nothing to others. Remember that it is what happens in the audience's mind, not what happens in yours, which counts. Unless you start from where they are, they will not understand. And if they do not understand they will switch off, they will not remember, they will not be influenced. In addition to specific knowledge in the audience's mind you will also use common patterns of knowledge as a basis for useful analogies, which serve as stepping stones to new knowledge. I have, for example, just used the analogies of the television documentary and the game of chess to make a particular point as clearly as possible.

Visuals to explain important or complex points

Pictures or diagrams can often be an aid to understanding. Used sparingly they can also contribute to the variety which many presentations need.

For example, the presenter who wants to make a vigorous point about market share might do so with an appropriate graph. Which do you think would be the most effective: reading off a list of market shares, or using a visual (Figure 10.3)? Notice that the visual is extremely simple because it is not a substitute for explanation, merely an aid. Detailed qualifications or significances would be given orally. A common mistake is to attempt to put too much information into a single diagram, and so add to confusion rather than subtract from it. The ideal is to use a single graph to make a single point, and to avoid showing a relationship between more than two factors. Thus it would be possible to show a relationship between market share and number of branch offices on one slide, and a relationship between market share and advertising budget on another. But to try to show both relationships on one visual could be confusing.

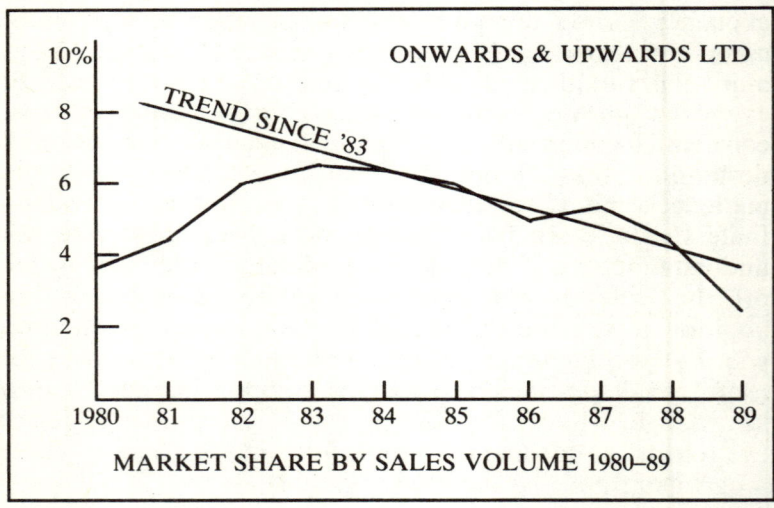

Figure 10.3   Better than a list of figures?

However, simplification must be used with care. It is very easy to distort the truth (without necessarily meaning to do so) in the interests of clarity. And the powerful impact which a visual can make only increases the danger.

A large company was in the habit of presenting its sales results in the form of a graph which, year by year, showed a gratifyingly upward slope. The effect of inflation was always mentioned but it was not until someone produced a

graph showing the sales figures adjusted for inflation that senior management realized that the slope was actually declining rather than ascending. They had vaguely suspected that this must be so, but it took the impact of the graph to ram the point home and lead to important changes in strategy.

Another form of visual which can assist understanding is one which illustrates an idea which might otherwise be too complex to grasp quickly. Figure 10.4 shows the use of the analogy as a stepping stone to new knowledge. However the picture cannot be grasped without the sort of explanation about analogies I have given above. In this case the picture might have been prepared in advance, but it could have been more effective if the presenter had actually drawn the picture as he gave his explanation. An overhead projector is excellent for this since the speaker can face the audience throughout. You do not need to be an artist to draw simple pictures, as my example shows, but you must have practised first. It may help to use prompt marks, invisible to the audience, to help you to get the positioning right.

Figure 10.4   Visual to assist understanding

Using variety

Variety is important for two reasons: it raises the attention level of the audience (remember, from Chapter 2, how the brain has a mechanism for directing attention to the new and dramatic), and it assists the absorption of the material. The extent and nature of the variety which a presenter should build in will depend on circumstances. A long presentation requires more variety than a short one; the type of variety used in a presentation to a general audience would differ from that used in a very businesslike presentation to a board of directors.

Variety of manner

The human voice carries a great deal of potential variety. It can be loud or soft, it can be fast or slow, it can change its pitch, it can use pauses. The human body can use a variety of stances and gestures; it can stand in different places. I am not suggesting that the presenter should be profligate with this kind of variety – there is always the danger of aping the mannered rhetoric which we associate with Victorian books on public speaking. But, in accordance with his personality and in harmony with the material he is presenting, a great deal of variety is possible. Ideally, the audience should not be directly conscious of this – they should certainly not see it as deliberate effect; all they are aware of is that this speaker is interesting to listen to, and holds their attention.

My wife and I were once asked to give a presentation to the senior class at a local school. Conditions precluded audience participation and we knew that the hour we had available was far too long to hold their attention. We adopted the device of alternating the material between us. The form teacher, who sat at the back, told us how she had watched the students lean forward with new interest whenever we changed speakers, gradually to relax back into passive listening until the other took over.

Variety of material

It is possible to give a plain presentation, factual, literal and complete. But most presentations are improved by judicious decoration. The good verbal illustration, a well told anecdote, a motivational story can all contribute to interest. Unless the presentation is very informal and with entertainment as a primary objective, these decorations should be clearly relevant to the matter in hand, and should contribute to the message. They should be well spaced, and used where the presenter feels that the audience needs a little rest, or where their attention may be flagging. Look particularly at the third quarter of a presentation when the audience is most likely to need reviving.

Steve Hindley, who heads the field management training programme at Sun Life of Canada, wanted to convince his audience of the value of role play as a training method. He chose to insert into his talk a short video recording of a role play taking place. While it was showing you could hear the audience of managers crackling with interest and comment as they recognized an all too familiar situation. Steve gained their attention, made his point, and gave them something to remember.

I have already spoken about the use of jokes to open a presentation, and I hesitate to mention humour as a decoration simply because the word has got about that a presentation without gusts of laughter is a failure. Certainly humour is a way of binding an audience through their shared laughter, and it gives variety and relaxation. But it is no more necessary than any other method of achieving variety; material which is intrinsically interesting and communicated in an interesting way has no particular need of humour to bolster it further. Some speakers have a flair for humour: let them use it, but let them be careful lest it is their humour which is remembered and not the substance. Other speakers have no flair for it: let them avoid it; there are many other ways of holding an audience.

Variety of method

The use of visuals, described above, is an example of variety of method. The audience is given something to do which is a change from listening. On a recent occasion I wanted to make a point about the rapid growth of office technology. I showed the audience a mechanical calculating machine; it was bulky and weighed about fifteen pounds. I told them that it had been in use only ten years before. I then showed them a cheap calculator about the size of a credit card, which had more power than its giant predecessor. Not only was the point made; I had given them some variety.

Variety of participation

Here is an example. I have transcribed it from a recording of an actual presentation:

'You've been listening to me for a few minutes now, and you will already have formed an impression about me. What do you guess my IQ is? You know that the average IQ is 100. Am I average, do you think? Above or below? Write the figure down on the corner of your programme. (Pause) No need to call any figures out, I haven't come here to be insulted. Done it? OK. Now the odds are that you have overestimated my IQ by 13 points. Why? Because (speaker takes off his glasses) on average people estimate someone wearing glasses at 13 more IQ points than the same person without. You see, what that suggests is that we often base our judgements about people on quite incidental and irrelevant things. And that means that we are often wrong.'

In some presentations it would be appropriate to have deliberate pauses for questions. If the audience has been given a clear structure they are unlikely to anticipate later stages of the presentation, but this can be reinforced by asking them to confine their questions to what has been said so far. It can be beneficial to ask an audience to pause and have a short discussion with their immediate neighbours. It might be put this way:

'We've looked at the three main strategies we've used in order to increase our market share. Let's pause for two or three minutes at this point. I'd like you to discuss with your immediate neighbours whether these strategies have anything in common – some common reason why they don't seem to have worked. (Speaker then sits down, and shows by reading his papers, that his audience is now expected to work.)

An easy method of gaining variety is to ask the audience to study a paper handout. This means a little pause while the paper is distributed and a period while the handout is being read. The information it contains might often just as easily have been shown on a screen, but the handout is *different*; it gives variety. Some presenters will go to considerable lengths to achieve variety. Haydn wrote a loud drum roll into his Surprise Symphony to gain the attention of his audience; and I remember how an audience in a hot London hotel were greatly enlivened by a bomb scare which obliged them to leave the room temporarily. When they returned they were lively when before they had been soporific, and attentive when before they had been bored. The bomb scare was not organized by the speaker, but it served him well.

An interesting experiment was carried out by a psychologist. He attached an instrument to record the heartbeat rate of members of an audience while they were given a lecture for an hour. The rate was high at the beginning, gradually dipped to a low level, and then recovered during the last few minutes. You may remember that recall of material follows the same pattern – high at the beginning and the end, low in the middle. Some weeks later the same audience members were given a lecture period in which a deliberate variety of methods was used, including some of those I have listed. The heartbeat rate increased every time the method was changed, and the audience retained a high average level of alertness (as measured by heartbeat) throughout. The lesson is obvious: if you want your audience to be alert and to listen in an active way, build in variety.[9]
But variety does not only gain attention; it also gains

retention. The methods I have described give the audience plenty of opportunities to rehearse what they have learnt. Sometimes this is achieved by simply giving them a natural break for reflection (while papers are being handed out, for instance); sometimes rehearsal is actually required from them (when they are asked to discuss a point together, or to ask questions, for instance).

A final word of warning. Don't overdo it. Speakers can become so preoccupied with variety that it becomes in itself a distraction. Decide how much variety your presentation really needs. Pick one or two methods which are the most appropriate to the occasion, and weave them naturally into your material. Remember that they are only a means of achieving your objective – not the objective itself.

Reversing the techniques

I have described the various techniques of the spoken presentation primarily with the object of showing how the speaker may make the most of his points through communicating them effectively to his audience. It follows that it is also in the speaker's power to play down the points which he does not want his audience to absorb; we have seen an example of this in looking at ways to time the introduction of contrary arguments so that they are least likely to loom large in the mind of the audience.

Because an audience is essentially passive, retains very little information unless it is helped to do so, and is unlikely to draw inferences for itself the presenter has considerable control over what is communicated. There is a moral question here. Socrates (or rather Socrates as interpreted by Plato, in his *Gorgias*) disapproves of oratory because it is concerned with convincing an audience rather than with teaching the truth. I do not propose to try to resolve this question here, but merely note that the speaker has a responsibility which is proportionate to his ability and opportunity to control the effect he has on the mind of his audience.

5 SPEAKING SKILLS

Creating audience contact is important, and the proper use of the eyes will help here. Good projection is another factor. Learn to use audience feedback.

The use of a script is damaging to audience contact. But for those who cannot do without, there are ways of alleviating the problem.

In general, preparation for a presentation is a lengthy task which cannot be skimped. Private rehearsal is essential. It is difficult to improve performance without a friendly, but honest, critic.

Audience contact

This chapter has been concerned with the aspects of constructing a presentation required to achieve maximum impact through motivation, meaning and memory. However, among the characteristics which distinguish the spoken from the written presentation, listed at the beginning of the chapter, was the relationship between the speaker and his audience; and the ability of the speaker to respond to the feedback he receives. A description of the factors which contribute to this cannot be a substitute for a live course in speaking skills, but it will explain why these skills are important to acquire.

Think back over some of the presentations you have heard. Many of them, though generally competent, will have made little impression on you. But there will have been a few which have seemed to have an extra quality – something hard to define, but related to the speaker's personality. You have felt drawn towards him, attracted to what he has to say; you may even feel that you somehow know him personally, even though that is impossible. Such a speaker has made a real, human contact with his audience. Now it is true that some people are blessed with strong, forceful personalities, and no account in a book, however many times it may be read, can convey that blessing. But the rest of us

must take pains to make sure that whatever personality we
do have is put across as effectively as possible when we are
presenting.

Defining your audience with your eyes

**Frank Sheed, who was one of the greatest orators ever to
appear at Speakers' Corner, Marble Arch, used to tell this
story. When he was a young man, a member of the Catholic
Evidence Guild, he was instructed to pick out a member of
his audience, standing somewhere towards the back of the
crowd, and to address his remarks to that person. On the
first occasion he was speaking on the subject of Hell; and
he fixed his eyes on a suitable-looking listener. As he waxed
emotional over his subject, he noted the listener's expression
change to one of horror. Soon he was trying to thrust himself
back into the crowd, but Frank, well instructed, kept him in
focus. Finally the listener escaped, and was last seen
sprinting away through Hyde Park as if all the demons of
Hell were at his heels.**

Frank quickly learnt that he had been wrongly instructed.
The speaker should look at his *whole* audience, allowing his
eyes to move around the perimeter, and around the centre,
and at those close to him. The movement should be natural;
he is not staring at them, but looking at them just as he
would look at someone he was addressing in day-to-day
conversation. His eyes will define his audience – those with
whom he is communicating personally.

Do not be put off because you cannot see the audience.
This occurs when a speaker is on a well-lit dais while the
audience is in darkness. Before the house lights go down
familiarize yourself with the shape of the audience, and then
look at them while speaking just as if you could see them.
They will not realize that you can't.

Projection

A speaker who defines his audience with his eyes will usually
project his voice well; it is instinctive to pitch the voice so

that it reaches the person one is looking at. A public address system is often provided nowadays for larger rooms, and this will take care of volume, provided it is adjusted correctly. Unless an operator is going to be available during the presentation, check on the adjustment beforehand. This is particularly important if you have a naturally quiet voice. A large room without a public address system can be more of a problem, but – unless it happens to be the Albert Hall – even a quiet voice will carry, provided enunciation and projection are good. It is quite in order to ask if people at the back can hear; and this in itself is a good way of establishing audience contact.

Projection is equally important for a very small audience but it is primarily a matter of stance and glance, rather than volume.

Audience feedback

All speakers are to some extent affected by a nervousness which makes thought processes difficult. In conversation we quite naturally think about what we are to say next and how the other person is reacting at the same time as we are speaking. Standing in front of an audience this capacity deserts us, and it is as much as we can do to get the right, carefully prepared, words out in the correct order. But with experience and a growing control over nervousness, the presenter will learn to recognize audience feedback and begin to respond to it. The most obvious signal is noise. Or rather lack of noise. A completely silent audience is a listening audience. A shuffling, creaking audience is bored and inattentive – action needs to be taken. If the house lights are up, then you will be able to watch expressions – nods from your allies, annoyed shakes from your opponents. But they're all listening.

Get rid of that script

It is clearly not possible to maintain audience contact when reading from a script. Looking up and grinning every paragraph or so will not disguise the fact that you are not speaking directly to the audience but merely conveying – as a tape recorder might – information dating from days, weeks or months before. There may be some practical advantages in giving the same material to a large body of people at the same time (see the beginning of this chapter) and therefore the paper designed to be read, to a learned society for example, has its place. But that is not what we are discussing.

For some people, though, the choice may not be there. If they cannot use a script they feel they cannot speak. If so, then it is at least possible to avoid the worst of the disadvantages by following two rules:

- Having planned the structure of the presentation along the lines I have suggested, lock yourself away in a room and start giving your presentation to an imaginary audience in your own words. Every two or three minutes write down what you have just said. Use a tape recorder if it helps. The point to notice is that the rhythms of natural speech are quite different from the rhythms of prose writing. By speaking first and recording afterwards your script will have speech rhythms.

- Set out your script so that you can read the text easily from a good distance, marking emphasis and pause points as required. Then practise giving the speech to an imaginary audience *several* times, so that you need only glance at the text during the actual presentation, reserving your main focus for the audience. Don't hesitate to alter the text during practice if you find other phrases coming more naturally.

Of course it is perfectly proper for the speaker who is relying only on notes to read material occasionally. No one is expected to have learnt quotes by heart, or to remember a row of figures. It may even be necessary to read a passage of a presentation verbatim if the exact phrasing is essential. Provided this is done only occasionally, with good reason and without concealment, it provides additional variety.

General preparation

Preparing for a presentation is a lengthy task. Having received my first lessons on public speaking as a junior at school I would regard myself, 40 years later, as quite experienced. Yet if I want to give of my best I still find that I require about 20 minutes total preparation time for every one minute of speaking. You may find that you take the same.

The later stages of preparation involve a great deal of rehearsal. Following decisions about structure and about the proper decoration of the speech you will be left with notes – sometimes several pages long. Eventually these notes will be boiled down to one page (although there may be supporting material such as quotations or statistics you intend to read). Some people prefer to put their notes on a number of cards; that is simply a personal preference.

The process of boiling down is carried out by rehearsal. Keep giving the speech as often as possible, only referring to your notes as necessary. I will rehearse while walking to the station, driving, and even in my bath – which lessens the temptation to have my notes too closely available. You will soon discover that your growing familiarity will enable you to reduce your notes to the very few points required to keep you on track. I like to use main headings corresponding to the structure, with sub-headings to remind me of the incidental points. You may like to have a rehearsal in front of a member of your family or a friend. This can be quite nerve-racking, but it often helps to relieve nervousness on the actual occasion.

Finally, have a last rehearsal on the day itself.

A friend indeed

The main difficulty which presenters have in improving their techniques is that it is hard to get constructive feedback. Most audiences will clap, and people will congratulate the speaker afterwards irrespective of his quality. This is why good public speaking courses involve plenty of practice and plenty of mutual criticism. A less satisfactory alternative – but a thousand times better than nothing – is to have a friend in the audience who will be prepared to give constructive criticism. It's painful to listen to such a friend telling you where you went wrong as well as where you excelled, but it's necessary. It is almost impossible to improve without accurate feedback, and the pain is a small price for becoming a competent presenter who is able to communicate his ideas effectively and persuasively.

Exhilaration

Yes, good speaking requires hard work. Planning, constructing, developing and rehearsing a presentation take time. And the wear on the nerves can be considerable. But there are few sensations as rewarding as knowing that you are giving a good presentation. The audience is listening raptly – and just to you; you are controlling their emotions and their thought processes; you are communicating new ideas with power; you are presenting yourself as a person of influence and consequence. It is the summit and the symbol of getting your own way in business.

REPORT WRITING

Good report writing is an important skill for anyone who seeks to persuade. A report may be used to introduce an idea to a Target, or to provide him with a text which he can study at leisure, or it may be the only way in which other people concerned in the decision get to know about the idea and the arguments for it. There are excellent books on the subject available, and examples are given in the Bibliography. This note is only intended to suggest how some of the points you have been studying in this book may be applied.

Earlier in this chapter I described some of the advantages of the spoken presentation over the written presentation. In particular I cited the reluctance of people to read, the ability of the speaker to define the pace and order of the material, and the opportunity the speaker has to adjust his presentation to the responses of his audience. I will look briefly at how the written presentation can address these potential difficulties; and I will do so always recalling that motivation, meaning and memory are as important for the reading audience as they are for the listening audience.

Getting the reader to read

Applying the motivation calculus (see the beginning of Chapter 3), your report will be read – or read with the attention it deserves – as a result of the balance between whether the reader wants the information, believes that the report will actually give it to him, and judges that the process of assimilation will be sufficiently easy. And this calculus will initially, and sometimes finally, be made when he receives the report. It will probably be based on the general form and feel of the report document, and on the contents of the first two or three pages.

The general feel and form of the report

Keep reports as short as they need to be, ruthlessly cutting any extraneous material. Many reports of national significance, sometimes resulting from a Royal Commission, have not needed to be more than 30 or 40 pages long, notwithstanding the complexity of the subject. Most business reports can be far shorter; if only one page is needed, then a two-page report is too long.

If appendices are required – perhaps to give detailed technical notes or lists of figures – bind these separately, or use tags which shows where they start. Many readers, often the most senior and influential, will not be interested in appendices. And even if they have to be sent to all, which is often not the case, the reader needs to see at once that he can grasp the information he needs from a briefer document. I have often set aside a thick report for reading on some leisurely occasion, hoping that it will never come, finally to discover that the report itself was short, and only the appendices voluminous.

Pay attention to the setting out of the report, using attractive headings and sub-headings. This makes the report, even at a glance, look both appealing to read and business-like. By convention, business reports are usually typed with single-line spacing, but short paragraphs with generous gaps and wide margins will relieve the eye and provide room for notes. Note taking will assist the reader's memory.

If the report contains graphs or illustrations insert these in the text (we all like a picture book) but keep them simple and immediately informative and interesting. The spirit of the rules for illustrations used in spoken presentations will apply, but there are some differences. These are explained in *Plain Figures* (see Bibliography) which is the best guide I know to the accurate and informative display of statistics, and has excellent notes on report writing. Never use computer printout in a report (you can do so in the appendices if necessary, but don't expect me to read it); in most instances the information is far too detailed for the body of the text but, if it has to be shown complete, put it through a word processor first so that it blends with the rest. Bind the report if it is of any length, but make sure it will open flat. There are many standard binding systems available, but choose an economical one to avoid conveying the impression that the high quality of the binding is intended to redress the low quality of the report.

The contents of the first two or three pages

What makes you want to read a newspaper story? Usually it's the headline. 'Nude vicar marries midget actress' will attract your eye. But if such extremes are not easily invoked for a business report at least use a title which will interest the reader and persuade him to look further. Compare for instance *A Report on Our Accounting Systems* with *Critical Factors in Our Accounting Systems, and how we can save money by changing them.* Which would you be more likely to want to read? In a very formal company you might need to use the second as a sub-title to the first, but make sure it's prominent.

The report should then continue with a brief summary of its contents. This may, in longer reports, refer to the numbers of the relevant sections. Such a summary should provide the reader with a good overall picture, and this has two purposes:

- Some readers will need to go no further. Either the report is irrelevant to them, or the summary gives them sufficient information. At least, in the latter case, they will have got the main message you wanted to communicate. Most newspaper stories continue down from the headline with a paragraph describing the main elements; fuller details come later. Journalists understand how people absorb information, so should you.

- A good summary will act as a strong encouragement to continue with the report. If the remarks induce curiosity or challenge the beliefs of the reader, he will want to know the evidence for them. But the evidence will only be found in the body of the report. So don't be afraid of a punchy, controversial summary – provided, of course, that adequate evidence is forthcoming.

Your summary will include your recommendations, or an adequately enticing reference to recommendations which appear later.

Primacy

Primacy applies to written reports, too, and constitutes a third reason for a good opening summary. While you cannot prevent your reader from starting at the back or in the middle, a well presented summary gives you the best chance of getting the right patterns fixed at the beginning so that later information will be noticed, interpreted and remembered in their light. Primacy can be used in the same way for the opening sentence or two of each section, which can itself be a mini-summary of what is to come.

Many reports will give an opportunity for the use of recency. For example, one report argued a close case between alternative courses of action. It ended with a section on tax effects which happened to give substantial advantages to one alternative. The reader who was asked to balance the arguments throughout the report was given a last push, calculated to ensure the acceptance of the final recommendation.

Structure

Structure plays the same part in a written presentation as it does in a spoken presentation (see p. 176 ff). If a report is to be understood and remembered it must follow logical patterns which aid meaning and recall. And these patterns must be clear to the reader so that the information he gleans can be easily related to them. A fourth reason for a good opening summary is that it does just this though, in some cases, a special directory to the report needs to be included.

Good layout reinforces structure, as well as being attractive. A sensible system of headings, sub-headings and perhaps sub-sub-headings should be used. Indentation and typestyles, italic for instance, can help. But avoid being fussy, or the temptation of showing just what a word processor can do. Use the minimum required to enable the structure to be clearly followed, and be consistent. Numbering sections or paragraphs can be useful if people are to comment on sections of the report, or if it is to be discussed in a group. Such a system can also help the report to look orderly and deliberate.

If you have difficulty in identifying your own structure when you come to write your opening summary or to decide about sub-headings, it simply means that you have written a muddled report out of a muddled mind. You must go back to your basic planning and decide what your structure is to be. Then revise your report, or start again. If *you* aren't clear your readers certainly won't be.

Style

Because business reports do not constitute literature (whatever that means) it is sometimes thought that fine writing is unnecessary. The contrary is true. Good style conveys the writer's exact meaning in a pleasing way. A business report often has far more consequences for people and money than conventional literature; precision of meaning is likely to be more important; pleasant reading, which holds the attention, is all the more needed when the matter is likely to be dry.

This is not the place for an instruction in good style, but some thoughts may be helpful:

- Your style cannot be better than your thinking. If you are clear about what you mean – not just in general but for every phrase you write – then you have a chance of communicating it clearly.

- Use a good book to guide you. My choice is *The Complete Plain Words* (see Bibliography). It is invaluable for the beginner, but many experienced writers – who know how easily bad habits reassert themselves – dip into it, or similar guides, often.

- Use a plain, clear style – simple words and short sentences. The clarity and force of the evidence and the ideas should be carrying the argument, not the emotion of the language. Avoid jargon, but you can use technical terms if these are familiar to your readers.

- Get into the habit of having your written work criticized by colleagues, and be ready to criticize theirs in return. A colleague will often notice an ambiguity, a carelessly written phrase or a muddled passage which has escaped the writer no matter what care he has taken. Both criticizing and being criticized are educational experiences.

Memorability

The tools for achieving memorability are fewer in written material than in spoken material – where pace, emphasis and drama are to hand. However, as I have described, primacy and recency can be used effectively. Well chosen visual illustrations are memorable because the visual imagination is captured and because study of the illustration commits it to the long-term memory. A point which would otherwise need lengthy explanation can often be simply communicated in this way.

There is room for a well turned phrase, which captures attention. But it gains force through being used sparingly, avoiding pretentiousness and the purple passage. Prefer the concrete statement buttressed by the concrete example to the woolly generality or the abstract phrase. Examples play the same role in writing as they do in speaking: they clarify meaning and they capture attention and memorability through the imagination.

A report should not be repetitious; this increases its length and tries the patience of the reader. But it is often possible to weave key ideas you wish to have remembered into later material in a different form – thus reinforcing without antagonizing. And some reports lend themselves to interim summaries which provide further opportunities.

Using this book

Most of the ideas suggested in this book can be adapted to the written report. A few examples will illustrate this. Having clear objectives remains just as important as for the spoken presentation. Knowing your audience and their expectations is even more so since you cannot adapt the report to the response of the reader. The patterns common to human nature, or particular to an individual, are present in the mind of the reader just as much as in the mind of the listener. If the brain is attuned to sudden rather than gradual change then a startling new fact can grab attention in just the same way. If fear is a powerful motivation you can appeal to it through the written word as well as the spoken. If a good analogy can alter the basis used for comparison, it will work as well on paper.

These methods continue to work, as I pointed out in Chapter 2, even when the Target is aware of what is happening. But the rational override (same chapter) is more likely to be invoked by the reader who has time to reflect or return to an idea. And a report should be seen as unbiased – any hint of the partisan endangers credibility. So the methods need to be employed with care and restraint; but they can be just as effective since the reader will have more time to absorb the force of their influence.

Conclusion

A book like this is really a form of long report, though it does not have that title. Thus you have the opportunity to consider whether I have been observing the points I have made on report writing. At the very least you have an immediate, though rather lengthy, example to hand to make your last comparison.

Summary

- The ability to give good spoken presentations is important for anyone who seeks to get his own way in business. Virtually everyone can become competent through observing the basic principles – but few do.
- Spoken presentations differ from written presentations in the following respects:

  – they enable information to be given to several people in the same way and at the same time;

  – the presenter has much greater control over the way in which the audience receives and retains information;

  – the presenter can make much more precise use of the patterns built into human beings, including the power of the group effect;

  – the presenter will make a much greater personal impact, for good or ill, on his audience.

- Start preparation by writing full objectives, including any ego objectives. Everything which follows must stem from these.

- Research your audience as much as you would an individual, but bear in mind the interplay within the group. In particular recognize the influential individuals, or groups; and consider their likely patterns.

- The separate points you will make and the structure of your presentation are interrelated. Keeping your objectives by you, develop ideas for your points over a period of time. Allow for random thinking, but be ready to prune ruthlessly.

- Since people rapidly forget information unless it is transferred to the long-term memory, observe the three principles of *motivation*, *meaning*, and *memory* in building your presentation.

- Design a simple and coherent structure, and announce this to your audience so that they have a pattern into which to slot the new information. Use sub-structures if the material is complex.

- Make use of the 'primacy' effect by establishing early rapport with your audience and giving them strong motivation to listen to you. This is your opportunity to set the pattern through which they will be most likely to interpret the presentation.

- Make use of the 'recency' effect by good summarizing, and leave your audience with a strong message which is important to your cause.

- If you need to deal with contrary arguments, use your knowledge of 'primacy' and 'recency' to place them within your structure so as to minimize their impact.

- The preferred pattern for making a point is *statement*, *example*, *inference*. This gives meaning, helps consolidation and guides the audience into the inference you wish them to draw. Remember how the choice of words or phrases can give an emotional overtone.

- The attention and the retention of the audience can best be ensured by providing variety (but don't overdo it), assisting meaning, and ensuring breaks for consolidation. Some ideas to bear in mind:

- use reminder visuals as a holding device to aid consolidation;

- help the audience to grasp new ideas by relating them to their existing ideas and patterns; remember the value of analogies;

- use visuals as an aid to explaining difficult ideas;

- use variety of delivery, voice and stance;

- use verbal illustrations, anecdotes, humour;

- use variety of methods, such as physical demonstration, audience participation, etc.

● Achieve good audience contact through use of the eyes, and projection. Learn to respond to audience feedback. If you have to use a script, develop it as a spoken, not a written, script.

● Boil down your original notes, through practice and rehearsal, so that they are no more than memory prompts.

● Use a good friend for constructive feedback.

● Written reports are another important medium for communicating your ideas. But special attention needs to be given to enticing the reader to read. Attractive appearance and a good opening summary will be important. The writer has less control over pace and order than the speaker but primacy and recency can still be applied. Structure, spelt out at the beginning and reinforced throughout by appropriate headings, will be important for meaning and memorability. Good writing style will be needed. Visual and verbal illustrations will give force, memorability and variety. Most of the ideas in this book can be adapted for written reports – and are just as effective in this form. But remember that the reader has more opportunity to use his automatic override and so care must be exercised.

References

Chapter 1

1. Greenberg, H. and Mayer, D. (1964), 'A new approach to the scientific selection of successful salesmen,' *The Journal of Psychology*, **57**, pp. 113–153.
2. Zajonc, R. B., Heingartner, A. and Herman, E. M. (1969), 'Social enhancement and the impairment of performance in the cockroach,' *Journal of Personality and Social Psychology*, **13**, pp. 83–92. Actually cockroaches are not great mathematicians anyway but, like human beings, they perform simple tasks better when watched by other members of their species – and more complex tasks worse.

Chapter 2

1. In my description of how the brain functions I have been much influenced by Professor Robert Ornstein (see Bibliography). But he must not be asked to take responsibility for my selection of his points, or for the inferences I have drawn from them.
2. There is even a mathematical equation proposed over 100 years ago by Ernst Weber to calculate at what point a change from the existing situation becomes just noticeable to the human senses.
3. Griffiths, I. (1988), *Creative Accounting*, Unwin Hyman.

4. Deaux and Wrightsman's *Social Psychology* (see Bibliography), pp. 104ff, gives a good account of pre-packaged judgements. These are known as *schemas* to psychologists.
5. Luchins, A. (1957), 'Primacy–recency in impression formation,' in Hovland, C. I. (ed.) *The order of presentation in persuasion*, Yale Univ. Press. Handy (see Bibliography), p. 78, reports a study by Kelley, H. (*Journal of Psychology*, 1950) in which an 'instructor' was introduced to classes either as a warm person or a cold person. The response of the class students to the instructor accorded with how they had heard him described.
6. Jones, E. E., Rock, L., Goethals, G. R., Shaver, K. G. and Ward, L. M. (1968), 'Pattern of performance and ability attribution: An unexpected primacy effect,' *Journal of Personality and Social Psychology*, **9**, pp. 317–40.
7. Quoted by Ornstein, p. 106.
8. Roberts, J. V. (1985), 'The attitude–memory relationship after 40 years: A meta-analysis of the literature,' *Basic and Applied Social Psychology*, **6**, pp. 221–41. Sweeney, P. D., and Gruber, K. L. (1984), 'Selective Exposure: Voter information preferences and the Watergate affair,' *Journal of Personality and Social Psychology*, **46**, pp. 1208–21.
9. Seligman, M. E. P. (1975), *Helplessness: On depression, development and death*, San Francisco, Freeman. And see Deaux and Wrightsman, pp. 235ff.
10. Snyder, M. and Swann, W. B. Jr. (1978), 'Hypothesis-testing processes in social interaction,' *Journal of Personality and Social Psychology*, **36**, pp. 1202-12.
11. Festinger, L. and Carlsmith, J. M. (1959), 'Cognitive consequences of forced compliance,' *Journal of Abnormal and Social Psychology*, **58**, pp. 203–10.
12. Even the rational override has its own patterns. People are more likely to accede to a request, such as allowing queue-jumping, if they are given a reason. But the relevance of the reason is not crucial – simply hearing the word 'because' is often sufficient to satisfy the need

to be rational. Langer, E., Blank, A. and Chanowitz, B. (1978), 'The mindlessness of ostensibly thoughtless action: The role of "placebic" information in interpersonal reaction,' *Journal of Personality and Social Psychology*, **36**, pp. 635–42.

Chapter 3

1. Carnegie, *How to Win Friends and Influence People* (see Bibliography), pp. 95, 96. Reproduced with permission.
2. Handy (1981), *Understanding Organizations* (see Bibliography), pp. 33, 36.
3. Heller (1985), *The New Naked Manager* (see Bibliography). See his chapter 'The motivational misfits' which criticizes motivational theorists, but, to my mind, leaves them largely intact – though with some usefully severe qualifications.
4. Maslow, A. (1943), 'A theory of human motivation,' *Psychological Review*, **50**, pp. 370–96. Brief accounts of Maslow, Hertzberg and McGregor can be found in Vroom and Deci (see Bibliography).
5. Hertzberg, F. (1966), *Work and the nature of man*, World Publishing Company.
6. McGregor, D. (1960), *The human side of enterprise*, McGraw-Hill.
7. Goffman (1959), *The Presentation of Self in Everyday Life* (see Bibliography).
8. Argyle (1972), *The Psychology of Interpersonal Behaviour* (see Bibliography).
9. Carnegie (see Bibliography), p. 165. Reproduced with permission.
10. Glass, D. C. and Singer, J. E. (1972), *Urban stress: Experiments on noise and social stressors*, New York, Academic Press, pp. 444, 584, 590.
11. Langer, E. J. and Rodin, J. (1976), 'The effects of choice and enhanced personal responsibility for the aged: A field experiment in an institutional setting,' *Journal of Personality and Social Psychology*, **32**, pp. 951–5. Rodin and Langer (1977), 'Long-term effects of a control-

relevant intervention with the institutionalised aged,' ibid., **35**, pp. 897–902.

12. Brehm, S. S. and Brehm, J. W. (1981), *Psychological reactance: A theory of freedom and control*, New York, Academic Press.

13. Quoted in Handy, p. 274.

14. Zuckerman, M. (1979), 'Attribution of success and failure revisited,' *Journal of Personality*, **47**, pp. 245–87.

15. Lerner, M. J. (1977), 'The justice motive,' *Journal of Personality*, **45**, pp. 1–52. Helen Reeves, director of National Association of Victim Support Schemes, commented to journalist Libby Purves (London *Times*, 3 October 1988): 'All of us need to believe that terrible things will not happen to us or our families. So when a girl is raped or murdered, something in us needs to believe that she was a prostitute; not like us.' Reproduced with permission.

16. Langer, E. J. (1975), 'The illusion of control,' *Journal of Personality and Social Psychology*, **32**, pp. 311–28.

17. Cialdini, R. B., Cacioppo, J. T., Bassett, R. and Miller, J. A. (1978), 'Low ball procedure for producing compliance: Commitment then cost,' *Journal of Personality and Social Psychology*, **36**, pp. 463–76

18. Bettger, *How I raised myself from failure to success in selling* (see Bibliography) p. 167.

19. See note 17. above.

20. Freedman, J. L. and Fraser, S. C. (1966), 'Compliance without pressure: the foot-in-the-door technique,' *Journal of Personality and Social Psychology*, **4**, pp. 195–202. DeJong (1979), 'An examination of self-perception mediation of the foot-in-the-door effect,' *ibid.*, **37**, pp. 2221–39.

21. Cialdini, R. B., Vincent, J. E., Lewis, S. K., Catalan, J., Wheeler, D. and Darby, B. L. (1975), 'A reciprocal concessions procedure for inducing compliance: The door-in-the-face technique,' *Journal of Personality and Social Psychology*, **21**, pp. 206–15.

22. Quoted in Handy, p. 213.

23. (1930). London, Chapman and Hall.

24. Quoted in Carnegie, p. 180, J. A. C. Brown (see

Bibliography) quotes a number of examples to illustrate this. For instance, a brewery making a light beer and a cheaper regular beer found that customers claimed to prefer the light to the regular by a margin of three to one. Sales showed that the regular beer outsold the light by nine to one.

Chapter 4

1. Chaiken, S. and Stangor, C. (1987), 'Attitudes and attitude change,' *Annual Review of Psychology*, **38**, pp. 575–630.
2. Barbara Tuchman in *The March of Folly* (1985, Sphere Books, London) describes many historical incidents, culminating in Vietnam, where the refusal of leaders or organizations to accept any facts which conflicted with their desires have so distorted the motivational calculus that disaster has been inevitable.
3. 'Market share' is a concept which delights the persuader. It is powerfully motivating (who doesn't want to increase market share?) but usually meaningless – or so elastic that it can be stretched to support or defeat any idea. According to your definition of the market your share can be seen to be very large or very small, whichever is convenient. Even used as a measurement over time, it does not measure your growth in absolute terms but only in relation to the whole, selected, market. Outside certain industries where degrees of domination are important, it doesn't tell you the only thing which really matters – whether you are profitable. It's better to be small and rich than large and broke.

Chapter 5

1. I am indebted to *Understanding Organizations* by Charles Handy (see Bibliography) for the broad classification of cultures into temples, networks and spiders' webs.

2. The label 'mystery culture' is my own coinage. The OED suggests that the old usage of 'mystery' to denote a skilled trade is related to 'mastery'; it is apt for the sub-culture I describe because it implies the possession of a special skill with overtones of exclusiveness and secrecy.
3. Handy, p. 80.
4. Deaux and Wrightsman, pp. 187–8, 247–8, and Atkinson, Atkinson and Hilgard, pp. 552–3, (see Bibliography) discuss a number of studies which relate similarity and liking to credibility, and the effects of familiarity on liking.
5. Discussed by Professor Donald Nicholl in *Clergy Review*, July 1964, pp. 393–415. He refers to Revans, R. W., (1964), *Standards for Morale: Cause and Effect in Hospitals*, Oxford University Press.

Chapter 6

1. Reported in the *Daily Telegraph*, 15 April, 1988.
2. Milgram, S. (1974), *Obedience to Authority*, New York, Harper & Row. About two-thirds of the subjects were prepared to give shocks up to, a supposed, 450 volts, and virtually none declined until the 'victim' had reached the stage of agonized screaming. Groups, asked to predict how many subjects would be prepared to go to 450 volts, estimated a proportion of 1–2 per cent.
3. Schjelderup-Ebbe, T. (1935), 'Social behaviour of birds' in Murchison, C. (ed.), *Handbook of Social Psychology*, Massachusetts, Clark University Press, pp. 947–72. Schjelderup-Ebbe's first observations of chickens' pecking order were conducted in 1913.
4. Knipe and Maclay (1972), *The Dominant Man* (see Bibliography), Chapter 3.
5. Knipe and Maclay, pp. 14–15.
6. Murchison, C. (1935), 'The experimental measurement of social hierarchy' in *Gallus domesticus*: Part III. *Journal of Genetic Psychology*, **46**, pp. 76–101.
7. Maslow, A. (1937), 'Dominance feeling, behaviour and status,' *Psychological Review*, **44**, pp. 404–29.

8. Wilson, P. R. (1968), 'The perceptual distortion of height as a function of ascribed academic status,' *Journal of Social Psychology*, **74**, pp. 97–102.

9. Doher, M. (1963), *Charles de la Bédoyère – aide de camp de L'Empereur*, Peyronnet, Paris.

10. Lefkowitz, M., Blake, R. R., and Mouton, J. S. (1955), 'Status factors in the violation of traffic signals,' *Journal of Abnormal and Social Psychology*, **51**, pp. 704–706.

11. Gough, H. G. (1957), *Manual for the California Psychological Inventory*, Palo Alto, Psychologists' Press.

12. Deaux and Wrightsman (see Bibliography) discuss the components of credibility as evidenced by studies, pp. 187–8.

13. Settle, R. B., and Gordon, L. L. (1974), 'Attribution theory and advertiser credibility,' *Journal of Marketing Research*, **11**, pp. 181–5

14. Stewart, J. E. (1980), 'Defendant's attractiveness as a factor in the outcome of trials,' *Journal of Applied Social Psychology*, **10**, pp. 348–61. Kulka, R. A. and Kessler, J. R. (1978), 'Is justice really blind? The effect of litigant physical attractiveness on judicial judgment, *Journal of Applied Social Psychology*, **4**, pp. 336–81.

Chapter 8

1. Goffman (1959) (see Bibliography).

2. Word, C. O., Zanna, M. P. and Cooper, J. (1974), 'The nonverbal mediation of self-fulfilling prophecies in interracial interaction,' *Journal of Experimental Social Psychology*, **10**, pp. 109–20.

3. For instance, Rosenthal, R. and Jacobsen, L. (1968), *Pygmalion in the classroom: Teacher expectation and intellectual development*. New York, Holt, Rinehart & Winston.

4. Sterling Livingston, J. (1969), 'Pygmalion in management,' *Harvard Business Review*, July/August. Reprint no. 69407. Reproduced with permission. Copyright 1969 by President and Fellows of Harvard College; all rights reserved.

5. Meyer, H. H., Kay, E. and French, J. R. P. (1965), 'Split roles in performance appraisal,' *Harvard Business Review*, January/February. Reprint no. 65108.

Chapter 9

1. Likert (1961) (see Bibliography).
2. Miller, D. (1968), *Using Behavioral Science to Solve Organization Problems*, International Personnel Management Association.

Chapter 10

1. Borden, R. J. (1980), 'Audience influence,' in Paulus, P. B., (ed.), *Psychology of Group Influence*, Hillsdale N. J., Erlbaum.
2. Deaux and Wrightsman (see Bibliography), pp. 405–10.
3. Gregg, V. (1975), *Human Memory*, Methuen.
4. Buzan, T. (1974), *Use Your Head*, BBC Publications, pp.44ff.
5. Miron, M. S. and Brown, E. R. (1968), 'Stimulus parameters in speech compression,' *Journal of Communication*, **18**, 3, pp. 319–25.
6. Chaiken, S. and Eagly, A. H. (1983), 'Communication modality as a determinant of persuasion: The role of communicator salience,' *Journal of Personality and Social Psychology*, **45**, pp. 241–56.
7. Karlins, M. and Abelson, H. I. (1970), *How Opinions and Attitudes are Changed*, New York, Springer, p. 22. Also Petty and Cacioppo (1981), *Attitudes and Persuasion: Classic and Contemporary Approaches*, Dubuque, 10, William C. Brown.
8. Rosenshine, B. (1965), 'Objectively measured behavioural prediction of effectiveness in explaining,' *California Technical Report, No. 4*. Stanford Research and Development Centre in Reading. And, for an audience's inability to draw inferences, Hovland, C. I. and Mandell, W. (1952), 'An experimental comparison

of conclusion-drawing by the communicator and the audience,' *Journal of Abnormal and Social Psychology*, **47**, pp. 581–8.

9. Bligh (1971), *What's the Use of Lectures?* (see Bibliography), pp. 183–4.

Select Bibliography

Bligh, Donald A., *What's the Use of Lectures?*, Penguin Education, 1972.
  This is an invaluable review of the research done on effective lecturing techniques. Essential for anyone who aspires to competence as a lecturer.
Carnegie, Dale, *How to Win Friends and Influence People*, Heinemann, 1986.
  If you have never read this book you have a revelation in store. If you have, read it again.
Chapman, Myra, *Plain Figures*, HMSO, 1986.
  An authoritative work on the display of statistics in tables, charts and diagrams; and their incorporation into reports.
Cialdini, Robert B., *Influence*, Scott Foresman, Illinois, 1988.
  Cialdini has made a special study of influence. His excellent book, already in its second edition, will probably become a classic. Available in the UK, but you may have to order.
Deaux, Kay and Wrightsman Lawrence S., *Social Psychology*, Brooks/Cole, Calif., 1988.
  A most useful textbook, surveying the whole field in a readable way. I am greatly indebted to it. Available in the UK.
Gowers, Sir Ernest (revised by S. Greenbaum and J. Whitcut), *The Complete Plain Words*, Penguin, 1987.
  If you aspire to good business writing this is all you need.
Handy, Charles B., *Understanding Organizations*, Penguin Education, 1981.

A comprehensive text, useful for anyone who wants to study what is known about organizations and their behaviour. Good bibliography for further study.

Knipe, Humphry and Maclay, George, *The Dominant Man*, Fontana, 1973.
The *British Journal of Psychiatry* described this as 'Complex research condensed into a form that can be easily assimilated.' I agree.

Machiavelli, Niccolo, *The Prince*, Rome, 1532.
If you haven't read this then you are 450 years out of date. There are always paperback translations in print.

Ornstein, Robert, *Multimind*, Macmillan, 1986.
This excellent book on mental processes started the train of thought which led me into print. Ornstein acknowledges his debt to Cialdini; and I – to both.

Wheatley, Doris, *Report Writing*, Penguin, 1988.
Covers the subject comprehensively for the beginner and for the experienced.

Other books to which reference is made.

Argyle, Michael, *The Psychology of Interpersonal Behaviour*, Pelican, 1972.

Atkinson, Rita A. and Richard C. and Hilgard, Ernest R., *Introduction to Psychology*, Harcourt Brace Jovanovitch, 1983.

Bettger, Frank, *How I Raised Myself from Failure to Success in Selling*, Heinemann, 1984.

Brown, J. A. C., *Techniques of Persuasion*, Pelican, 1977.

de la Bedoyere, Quentin, *Managing People and Problems*, Gower, 1988.

Goffman, Erving, *The Presentation of Self in Everyday Life*, Pelican, 1959.

Harvard Business Review, Reprint Service, Box 100, Soldiers Field, Boston MA 02163, USA.

Heller, Robert, *The New Naked Manager*, Hodder & Stoughton, 1985.

Honey, John, *Does Accent Matter?*, Faber & Faber, 1989.

Jay, Antony, *Corporation Man*, Jonathan Cape, 1972.

Likert, Rensis, *New Patterns of Management*, McGraw-Hill, 1961.

Townsend, Robert, *Up the Organization*, Fawcett Crest, 1970.

Vroom, Victor H. and Deci, Edward L., *Management and Motivation*, Penguin Education, 1970.

Relaxation and non-verbal communication.

Argyle, Michael, *Bodily Communication*, Methuen, 1975.

Benson, Herbert, *The Relaxation Response*, Collins, 1975.

Martin, Ian C., *The Art and Practice of Relaxation*, Hodder & Stoughton, 1977.

Nierenberg, Gerard I. and Calero, Henry H., *How to Read a Person Like a Book*, Heinrich Hanau, 1973.

Index